Counseling
Survivors of
Childhood
Sexual Abuse

Counselling in Practice

Series editor: Windy Dryden
Associate editor: E. Thomas Dowd

Counselling in Practice is a series of books developed especially for counsellors and students of counselling which provides practical, accessible guidelines for dealing with clients with specific, but very common, problems.

Counselling Survivors of Childhood Sexual Abuse

Claire Burke Draucker

SAGE Publications
London • Thousand Oaks • New Delhi

First published 1992 Reprinted in 1993, 1994

SAGE Publications Ltd
6 Bonhill Street
London EC2A 4PU

SAGE Publications Inc
2455 Teller Road
Thousand Oaks, California 91320

SAGE Publications India Pvt Ltd
32, M-Block Market
Greater Kailash – I
New Delhi 110 048

British Library Cataloguing in Publication Data

Draucker, Claire Burke
    Counselling Survivors of Childhood Sexual Abuse. –
    (Counselling in Practice Series)
    I. Title II. Series
    362.7

    ISBN 0–8039–8570–3
    ISBN 0–8039–8571–1 (pbk)

Library of Congress catalog card number 92–050478

Typeset by Mayhew Typesetting, Rhayader, Powys
Printed in Great Britain by the Cromwell Press Ltd.,
Broughton Gifford, Melksham, Wiltshire

Contents

1

Introduction

The experience of childhood sexual abuse is often a significant trauma that may continue to have an impact on survivors throughout their life span. Therefore, when adult survivors of childhood sexual abuse seek counseling, whether or not the sexual abuse is the presenting concern, counselors must be prepared to explore with them the role this experience has played in their development and the effect the abuse might be having on their present concerns. Due to the prevalence of childhood sexual abuse in the histories of individuals who seek counseling and the possible pervasive and long-term effects that stem from the abuse, it is important that all counselors become adept at addressing the unique and complex needs of survivors.

This chapter will address several basic issues related to the phenomenon of childhood sexual abuse. Topics include the definition of childhood sexual abuse, the recognition of sexual abuse as a significant social problem, and empirical research findings related to adult survivors. In addition, several fundamental counseling issues are addressed and the structure of the book is outlined.

Definitions of childhood sexual abuse

Defining childhood sexual abuse has been problematic for both researchers and clinicians. Definitions in the literature vary according to the types of activities considered to be 'sexual' and to circumstances considered to constitute abuse. All forms of sexual activity involving genital contact for either the offender or the victim, such as genital fondling and vaginal, anal, and oral intercourse, are usually included in definitions of sexual abuse. Also typically included are other forms of direct, physical sexual contact, such as fondling of the breasts, buttocks, or thighs and sexual kissing.

In some instances, definitions of childhood sexual abuse include non-contact sexual activities (Benward and Densen-Gerber, 1975; Finkelhor, 1979; Meiselman, 1978). These activities could include overt requests by the offender for sexual activities (e.g., a father asking his daughter to have intercourse with him), deliberate exposure of the offender's sex organs, or exposure of the victim's sex organs for the offender's sexual gratification. Non-contact sexual activities could also include incidents in which victims are photographed nude or in suggestive sexual poses for the offender's sexual gratification or for other exploitative purposes (such as money) or when victims are deliberately made to witness adult sexual activities. Blume (1986: 5) stated that sexual abuse 'does not require penetration, nor does it even require touch: it can occur through genital or non-genital fondling, or in the way a child is talked to, what the child is forced to see, hear, or do with others. It is the use of a minor to meet the sexual or sexual/emotional needs of another person.' However, including non-contact sexual activities in the definition of sexual abuse is controversial. Some authors have suggested that because non-contact sexual experiences are not experienced in the same way as are acts that involve actual physical violations of the child's body, and are less likely to result in long-term harm (Peters et al., 1986), these acts should not be included in general definitions of childhood sexual abuse. Others argue that because these experiences are nonetheless exploitative, they are often experienced as traumatic and should therefore be considered sexual abuse incidents. Some researchers (e.g. Russell, 1986) have dealt with this issue by differentiating between contact and non-contact sexual activities in empirical studies.

Another controversial issue is determining what factors make a sexual experience abusive. All situations in which physical force or threat of harm are used are typically considered abusive, as are situations in which the offender wields power over the victim due to older age or an authoritative position. Most would agree, for example, that non-coerced sexual exploration between peers or siblings close in age does not constitute abuse. Who might be considered a more 'powerful' other is debated. Some empirical researchers have specified that a certain disparity between the age of the victim and the age of the offender is necessary to constitute abuse (e.g., 5 years for a child victim, 10 years for an adolescent victim) (Peters et al., 1986). However, other factors might also contribute to a difference in power between the victim and the offender. For example, an offender may enjoy greater authority in a family, regardless of age, because he is considered the 'favorite son.' Sexual activity perpetrated by such individuals may be perceived by sibling victims as abusive because the offender had power over them due to family roles.

When the childhood sexual abuse is specified as 'incestuous,' another criterion issue arises. Typically, incest is legally defined as sexual activity between two individuals with blood ties that prohibit marriage. However, this definition is too narrow to be clinically relevant. While most clinical definitions of incest do include sexual activities between close relatives by blood, marriage, or adoption, there is some discrepancy regarding the inclusion of other relationships. Blume, for example, indicated that offenders of incest include anyone who has power over the child due to trust or authority when there is a 'bonding or surrogate parent relationship' (1986: 5). According to Blume this could include a babysitter, a teacher, or a parish priest. Others argue that including such extra-familial individuals in the definition of incest might mask the prevalence of abuse at the hands of a father, stepfather, or brother, which is thought to be particularly devastating (Hall and Lloyd, 1989).

As the purpose of this book is to deal with childhood sexual abuse as a counseling concern, a broad definition, based on clinical relevance, will be employed. Therefore, childhood sexual abuse is considered to include any exploitative sexual activity, whether or not it involves physical contact, between a child and another person who by virtue of his or her power over the child due to age, strength, position, or relationship uses the child to meet his or her sexual and emotional needs. Although variables such as the closeness of the relationship and the type of sexual activity involved do seem to be related to the degree of trauma, the adult survivor's perception of the experience as traumatic and a determination of the impact it has had on his or her life are of greatest interest to counselors in defining an abusive childhood sexual experience.

The recognition of sexual abuse as a significant social problem

The counseling of adult survivors of childhood sexual abuse has long been hindered by the denial of this phenomenon. Herman (1981) discussed the response of the public and of professionals historically to reports of childhood sexual abuse. She outlined three historical 'discoveries' of the prevalence of sexual abuse in our society.

The awareness of the occurrence of sexual abuse as a traumatic experience in the lives of children is usually traced to Freud (Herman, 1981), who is credited with the first 'discovery' of incest. When female patients in large numbers revealed to Freud that they had had childhood sexual experiences with adult men in their families, Freud, in what became known as the seduction theory, initially suggested that these traumatic experiences were the cause of hysteria. In the service of protecting the patriarchal family structure, Freud identified the perpetrators of the sexual abuse as other children, caretakers, or more distant relatives, but not fathers. In response to peer pressure, however, eventually Freud completely repudiated the seduction theory and claimed instead that his patients' frequent reports of sexual abuse were incestuous fantasies rather than actual childhood events.

For decades following Freud's repudiation of the seduction theory, Herman reports, professionals maintained a 'dignified silence' (1981: 10) on the topic of incest and the public continued to deny the reality and the prevalence of childhood sexual abuse. It was not until the 1940s that incest was 'discovered' for a second time by social scientists conducting large-scale survey studies of sexual practices, including the now famous Kinsey study (Kinsey et al., 1953). These studies documented that between 20 percent and 30 percent of the women who responded to the surveys reported having had a sexual experience as a child with a male, between 4 percent and 12 percent reported a sexual experience with a relative, and 1 percent reported a sexual experience with a father or stepfather. The sexual abuse of boys was not addressed in several of these studies, although one researcher (Landis, 1956) reported that 30 percent of the male participants in his survey reported a childhood sexual experience with an adult, who was most typically a male.

Although the prevalence of childhood sexual abuse was substantiated in these studies, the reality of the phenomenon continued to be denied by both the researchers and the public. For example, most of the sexually abused women in the Kinsey study reported being disturbed by the experience, and yet the researchers indicated that the women's distress resulted not from the sexual act itself, but from their social conditioning. Herman concluded that Kinsey and his colleagues, in their attempt to encourage enlightenment and tolerance of sexual attitudes, 'failed to distinguish between essentially harmless acts committed by consenting adults, "nuisance acts" such as exhibitionism, and frankly exploitative acts such as the prostitution of women and the molesting of children' (1981: 17).

Herman (1981) dated the 'third discovery' of incest to the 1970s and credited the feminist movement with bringing the problem of childhood sexual abuse, along with other taboo issues such as wife-battering and rape, into public awareness. This was followed by legitimate, scientific studies of the problem and public revelations of incest survivors who chose to tell their stories. However, although the feminist movement has done a great deal to break

through centuries of denial, the historical legacy of denial inevitably continues to have an impact on the attitudes of survivors and on the attitudes of those who counsel them.

Empirical research related to childhood sexual abuse

Current research related to childhood sexual abuse has focused primarily on determining the prevalence of abuse in the population and in clinical subgroups, identifying long-term effects that stem from the abuse, relating specific abuse characteristics to long-term effects, and exploring what factors might mediate the relationship between abuse characteristics and adult functioning. As many of these issues are pertinent to counseling survivors, this research will be briefly reviewed and summarized.

Prevalence

Researchers now generally agree that the occurrence of childhood sexual abuse is much more frequent than originally believed. However, studies have reported a wide variation in prevalence rates, that is the proportion of the population who have experienced childhood sexual abuse. For example, Peters et al. (1986), in a review of childhood sexual abuse prevalence studies conducted in North America, reported prevalence figures ranging from 6 percent to 62 percent for female samples and from 3 percent to 31 percent for male samples. These differences are presumably due to the way sexual abuse is operationally defined (e.g. the types of sexual activities included), the characteristics of the sample studied (e.g. college samples versus national random samples), and variations in research methodology (e.g. face-to-face interviews versus surveys). However, in a study with a random sample of 930 women in San Francisco, Russell (1986) reported that 54 percent of the participants had experienced at least one incident of sexual abuse prior to the age of 18, when incidents involving both intra-familial and extra-familial perpetrators, and contact and non-contact sexual activities, were included. Murphy (1989), using a similarly broad definition of childhood sexual abuse, conducted a telephone survey of 777 men in Minnesota, and reported that 11 percent had experienced an incident of sexual abuse by the age of 18. Therefore, although research limitations and discrepancies among studies result in varied estimates, large-scale studies such as these do suggest that a significant portion of the population have experienced at least one incident of childhood sexual abuse as children.

Researchers have also begun to document a high rate of sexual abuse in the histories of certain clinical populations. Studies of psychiatric populations, for example, suggest that between 26 percent and 40 percent of in-patients and out-patients have experienced childhood sexual abuse (Carmen et al., 1984; Jacobson, 1989; Jacobson and Herald, 1990; Rosenfeld, 1979). So childhood sexual abuse is both a major social and clinical problem and it is safe to estimate that a large proportion of individuals who seek counseling will have had some experience of childhood sexual abuse.

Long-term effects
Just as the prevalence of childhood sexual abuse has historically been denied, the long-term effects thought to stem from experiences of sexual abuse have been minimized. There are some who continue to maintain that sexual activity between a child and an adult is harmless. Ramey (1979), for example, suggested that incest could have beneficial results if it were not for society's negative reactions to it.

Clinicians, as well as researchers conducting descriptive studies, have maintained, however, that experiences of childhood sexual abuse often result in many long-term effects. These effects include sexual dysfunction; depression, suicidality, and guilt; isolation and disturbed interpersonal relationships; post-traumatic stress symptomatology; physical, sexual, or emotional victimization; substance abuse and other self-destructive behavior; and various somatic complaints (Benward and Densen-Gerber, 1975; Britcher, 1986; Forward and Buck, 1978; Gordy, 1983; Gross et al., 1980; Tsai and Wagner, 1978; Van Buskirk and Cole, 1983). Because many of these effects were observed in therapy populations or in small clinical research samples, it is difficult to document which effects stem from the abuse experience itself and to determine the effects of sexual abuse on survivors who do not seek the services of clinicians.

Research studies employing control groups of individuals who have not been sexually abused and studies using non-clinical samples have also begun to document these long-term effects. Adult victims of childhood sexual abuse, when compared to similar, non-abused individuals, have demonstrated more marital and family conflict and physical and sexual problems (Meiselman, 1978); more adolescent turbulence (Herman and Hirschman, 1981); less sexual activity and greater amounts of sexual anxiety, guilt, and dissatisfaction (Langmade, 1983); more guilt related to sexual issues (McBride, 1984); more life trauma, more sexual dysfunction, a higher level of stress during recovery from alcoholism, and a younger age of onset

of problem drinking (Kovach, 1983); and more depression, lower
self-esteem, less assertiveness, more sexual dysfunction, and more
physical/sexual abuse (McCord, 1985). Studies utilizing psychological assessment instruments, such as the Rorschach or the
Minnesota Multiphasic Personality Inventory (MMPI) have also
demonstrated higher degrees of psychological distress in groups of
women and men who have been sexually abused when compared to
those who had not (Meiselman, 1980; Olson, 1990; Owens, 1984;
Roland et al., 1985; Roland et al., 1989; Scott and Thoner, 1986).

There is increasing evidence that community samples, as well as
clinical samples, report negative long-term effects from their experiences of childhood sexual abuse. For example, in a non-clinical,
community sample of 152 incest survivors, half reported they had
suffered 'substantial lasting effects' from the abuse and 27 percent
reported that the abuse had a 'great effect' on their lives (Herman
et al., 1986). Of the women who experienced incestuous sexual abuse
in Russell's (1986) community sample of 930 women in San Francisco, 34 percent reported extreme trauma, 23 percent reported con-
siderable trauma, 25 percent reported some trauma, and 18 percent
reported no trauma stemming from their abuse experience.

Browne and Finkelhor, in a comprehensive review of the
empirical literature related to the impact of childhood sexual
abuse, concluded, 'When studied as adults, victims as a group
demonstrate impairment when compared to their non-victimized
counterparts, but under one-fifth evidence serious psychopathology' (1986: 72). This was similar to the conclusion reached
in an earlier review by Herman: 'The preponderance of evidence
suggests that for any child, sexual contact with an adult, especially
a trusted relative, is a significant trauma which may have long-
lasting deleterious effects. The sexual trauma does not necessarily
lead to the development of a major mental illness' (1981: 33).

Although the conclusion that childhood sexual abuse leads to
severe psychopathology is unjustified, research does support the
view that experiences of childhood sexual abuse increase the like-
lihood that survivors will suffer some negative effects later in life.
These effects are most commonly depression, post-traumatic symptomatology, interpersonal and/or sexual difficulties, and increased
risk of further abuse by self (e.g. substance abuse) or others.

Characteristics of the abuse situation and long-term effects

Researchers have attempted to relate specific characteristics of the
abuse situation itself – such as the use of force, the age of the

offender and the age of the child at the time of the abuse, the child's degree of relatedness to the offender, the offender's gender, the invasiveness of the sex act, and the duration of the experience – to long-term effects. Finkelhor (1979) found that the use of force and the age of the offender were related to the survivors' perceptions of the negativity of the sexual abuse. Silver et al. (1983) reported that the older the victim was at the termination of the incest and the longer the duration of the experience, the more frequent was the search for meaning in the event, which in turn resulted in psychological distress. In their study involving a community sample of incest survivors, Herman et al. (1986) reported that the use of force, the degree of physical violation, the duration of the abuse, the age difference between the offender and victim, and the nature of the relationship between the victim and the offender (e.g. father or stepfather versus other relatives) all contributed to the participants' perceptions of the negative impact of the experience on their lives. Peters (1988), in her study of 119 women in the Los Angeles area, reported that for those women who had been sexually abused the number of contact abuse incidents was the most significant predictor of the degree of psychological distress in adulthood, followed by the duration of the abuse and being older when the last abuse incident occurred. Lack of maternal warmth was also related to psychological difficulty. In a sample of 1500 nurses, Greenwald and Leitenberg (1990) found that post-traumatic stress symptoms were more likely to occur and were more severe in women who were sexually abused by fathers or who had experienced abuse in which intercourse was completed or attempted. In a study involving a large community sample, Finkelhor et al. (1989) reported that if the sexual abuse involved penetration, the survivors were more likely to report marital disruption, dissatisfaction with sexual relationships, and a greater tendency not to practice religion.

Results of these studies vary somewhat regarding which specific aspects of the abuse situation seem to cause the most trauma. However, it seems that abuse by a close relative, such as a father or stepfather; more 'severe' abuse, that is sexual activities which are invasive, long-lasting, and accompanied by force; and the relative powerlessness of the child, due to factors such as age disparity between victim and offender, all seem to be related to the degree of trauma experienced by the victims of childhood sexual abuse.

Mediating factors

A few studies have begun to examine factors that might mediate the effects of abuse situation characteristics on long-term adjustment.

One example of a mediating factor is the way survivors, as adults, cognitively process and respond to the abuse situation. Gold (1986), for example, tested the learned helplessness model of depression (Abramson et al., 1978) with a community sample of 103 survivors of childhood sexual victimization. The basic assumption of this model, that individuals' causal attributions mediate their responses to traumatic situations, was supported as the survivors' internal, global, and stable attributional style for bad events was related to poor adult functioning. Gold concluded that the coping difficulties exhibited by many survivors may be related to their attributional style. In a study of 77 adult women survivors of father–daughter incest, Silver et al. (1983) investigated the relationship between the survivors' ability to find meaning in the incest experience and adult functioning. It was assumed that the process of finding meaning can restore one's beliefs in an orderly, predictable, and fair world, beliefs that are threatened by a traumatic event. The authors found that the ability to find meaning in the incest experience did facilitate coping in this sample. Those survivors who reported making sense out of their experience reported less psychological distress, better social adjustment, higher self-esteem, and greater resolution of the incest experience. Taylor has suggested that adjustment to threatening events centers around three themes: 'a search for meaning in the experience, an attempt to regain mastery over the event in particular and one's life more generally, and an effort to enhance self-esteem – to feel good about oneself again despite the personal setback' (1983: 1161). Draucker (1989), in a study of 142 female incest survivors, discovered that successful accomplishment of these three tasks was related to three indices of adult adjustment including less depression, greater self-esteem, and greater social role functioning.

Although this line of research is in its infancy, it does seem to suggest that there are certain cognitive processes, which, if used by adult survivors, might reduce the harmful effects of childhood sexual abuse. Identifying such intervening variables may aid counselors in treatment planning by pointing to coping mechanisms that aid in recovery.

Principles of counseling adult survivors are therefore based on research that suggests that childhood sexual abuse is prevalent in the population and in the histories of those who seek counseling and that it often results in long-term effects. In addition, certain characteristics of the abuse situation are related to long-term effects, but these relationships can be mediated by certain psychological processes employed by survivors. As Herman stated, 'To be sexually exploited by a known and trusted adult is a central and formative experience in the lives of countless women' (1981: 7). It is now also believed that the same could be said about the lives of countless men (Urquiza and Keating, 1990).

Basic counseling issues

When discussing the counseling of adult survivors of childhood sexual abuse, several basic issues or questions arise. Although there are no definitive answers to these questions, each will be addressed in turn.

Counselor qualifications

One question often asked by counselors is whether the unique needs of the adult survivor require that he or she be seen by a sexual abuse 'specialist,' a professional who works with adult survivors as a primary clinical focus. If we continue to find that as many as 40 percent, or more, of individuals in treatment have had some experience of childhood sexual victimization, it is unlikely that all of these clients can be seen by a 'specialist.' More importantly, while it is important for counselors to recognize survivors' needs as unique and complex, to suggest that they therefore need to see a 'specialist' might well reinforce the survivors' perceptions of their needs as extremely complicated or unusual, thereby increasing their sense of isolation and their view of themselves as being different.

However, counselors do need to develop skills and competencies to meet the needs of survivors effectively. For example, the development of self-awareness regarding one's attitudes and beliefs related to the issue of childhood sexual abuse is essential. As mentioned earlier, helping professionals come from a tradition of denial of the reality and prevalence of childhood sexual abuse. Seemingly, this reflects deeper societal values regarding gender roles, power issues, and the rights of children. Counselors need the skills of reflection to examine their personal values and to determine any attitudes they might hold (e.g. denial, disgust, blaming the victim) that could interfere with effective counseling. Counselors must also question whether they continue to accept any myths that research and clinical experience have consistently disproved. Hall and Lloyd (1989), for example, have outlined certain myths related to sexual abuse that are still held by many. These include the belief that sexual abuse occurs only in certain subgroups of the population (e.g. poor, isolated families), that if a child does nothing to stop the abuse he or she must therefore have welcomed it, and that mothers often 'collude' with the abuser and so share responsibility for the abuse.

In addition to evaluating their beliefs and attitudes, counselors do need training and supervision in counseling adult survivors. A counselor who is inexperienced in dealing with this clinical issue needs to develop and maintain competencies as one would when faced with any special clinical concern (such as treating substance abuse or counseling individuals from varied cultural backgrounds). Training can occur through both classroom or workshop instruction and supervised clinical experience. In addition, because counseling survivors can be an intensely emotional experience that can provoke numerous personal issues for the counselor, supervision or professional consultation is recommended even for counselors who are experienced in this area.

The counselor's gender
Another question that frequently arises is whether counselors should be of the same gender as the survivors with whom they are working. As female survivors seek counseling more frequently and have traditionally been the focus of the clinical literature, the question most often posed is whether female survivors should be seen by female counselors. While many clinicians identify the benefits to survivors of both female and male counselors, some have concluded that, at least initially, a female counselor is preferable. Cole (1985), for example, took a strong stance advocating the use of female therapists in survivor groups. She stated, 'Female group leaders decrease the chances of revictimization of the client. Male therapists may quite inadvertently revictimize incest survivors due to their own male enculturation and client's lack of knowledge and skill in setting emotional and physical boundaries with men' (1985: 81). Faria and Belohlavek (1984) suggested that while a male therapist would allow survivors to learn to develop healthy relationships with men, a female counselor is preferable as she can serve as a role model. Blake-White and Kline (1985) argued that female therapists are more effective as leaders of incest therapy groups as it is usually easier for survivors to trust women. These authors also pointed out that survivors may 'perform for' and 'give away power' (1985: 399) to men. However, they have recommended that a male co-therapist, introduced at a later point, could benefit the group as this would provide the survivors with an opportunity to explore their attitudes toward men. Hall and Lloyd (1989), while identifying the advantages of a female counselor, also acknowledged that if trust can be established with a male counselor, the survivor has the advantage of being able to establish a healthy relationship with a male. Others maintain that the gender of the counselor is not a significant issue. For example,

Westerlund (1983) emphasized that the counseling style is more influential than the gender of the counselor in determining how issues of power are handled within the relationship.

Hall and Lloyd (1989) identified issues that might serve as potential difficulties for counselors of each gender. A female counselor, for example, may overidentify with survivors' issues, become overinvolved with their problems, and play the role of the 'rescuer.' Male counselors, on the other hand, might overidentify with the abuser, focus on issues of sexuality rather than abuse of power, or feel guilty about being male and attempt to overcompensate for this by being 'kind' to the survivor.

Less has been written regarding the gender of counselors with male survivors. Bruckner and Johnson (1987), who discussed group treatment for adult male survivors of sexual abuse, recommended the use of a mixed-gender team as co-leaders because having a female present in their groups seemed to facilitate the discussion of issues and feelings, although the participants also seemed to seek the female co-leader's acceptance and permission. Evans, who discussed the treatment of male sexual assault survivors and Vietnam veterans, stated that, 'The key issue in gender identification with the client . . . is not the gender of the client and the survivor but the gender attitudes' (1990: 71). Counseling is hindered by male gender stereotyping resulting in harmful beliefs (for example that male survivors are more to blame for their abuse than are females, males are unable to address personal issues, males are more competent and therefore male survivors are less in need of treatment than are female survivors).

So the literature recommends that a female counselor may be more effective, at least initially, in working with female survivors, although there are also some advantages to including a male therapist at some point in the process. Clinicians working with male survivors have not taken a similar stance (i.e. that male survivors should be seen by male counselors). However, in general, counselors' ability to examine their own gender-related issues as these influence their beliefs and attitudes, and the ways in which power issues are handled within the counseling relationship, may ultimately be more important that the gender mix between counselor and client.

The gender of the client
Another key issue to be addressed is the differences in the counseling process for male and female survivors. Again, because traditionally the focus has been on the counseling need of the female survivor, the question most commonly raised is how the counseling

needs of males differ from those identified for females. Because many female and male responses to childhood sexual abuse are similar (e.g. guilt, shame, anger), in some respects many counseling processes and techniques to be discussed are applicable to both genders. But as the socialization of males and females differs, it can be expected that males will be confronted with different sexist biases, exhibit gender-specific presentations of symptoms, and have specific treatment needs (Hunter and Gerber, 1990).

Urquiza and Capra (1990), in their review of the initial and long-term effects of childhood sexual abuse on boys, cited several effects that were similar to those experienced by women and girls (e.g. self-concept disturbance, somatic complaints) but identified two areas which 'stood out' for males: disturbances of conduct and acting out of compulsive sexual behaviors. The authors suggested that these effects are related to gender-based differences in coping with trauma, most specifically the use of externalizing behaviors by males. Struve (1990) suggests that the recovery of male survivors is influenced by their socialization, which leads them to believe that they should not be victims, that they can act on their feelings but not express them, and that they should have been able to protect themselves from their abuse.

Abuse by member of the same sex
A closely related issue is that of same-sex versus opposite-sex abuse. It is still generally believed that the sexual victimization of female victims by male perpetrators is the most common form of abuse. However, it is believed that males are the most frequent offenders against boys.

In addition to addressing the impact of socialization on males' responses to victimization, the issue of same-sex abuse is also pertinent. The most frequently discussed specific effect arising from the experience of male-to-male abuse is confusion related to sexual identity. Struve (1990) pointed out, for example, that if the abused boy perceives himself as experiencing pleasure or sexual arousal, which are normal physiological responses to stimulation, he may interpret those reactions as latent homosexual feelings and this can lead to later identity confusion. Some researchers have found a relationship between sexual victimization by an older male in childhood and later same-sex behaviors (Finkelhor, 1979). The male survivor often directs anger towards himself for not protecting himself from the offender and therefore views himself as 'less of a man' (Struve, 1990). He may then try to overcompensate for this failure, resulting in exaggerated 'macho behaviors,' homophobia, sexually aggressive behaviors, and, in some cases, sexual offending.

Counselors of male survivors need to be sensitive both to gender-specific issues of abuse and to issues related to same-sex abuse.

As Sepler pointed out, male victims inevitably experience their abuse from a different world view and self-view than do females. She warned counselors that a crisis experienced by the male survivor related to the abuse 'may be unresponsive to, or further precipitated by, a program model that assumes universality when it comes to sexual victimization' (1990: 76). For example, because males are raised to value mastery, they may be unlikely to acknowledge their powerlessness in the situation in the way that females might, and adapt by adopting a 'pseudoconsensual posture or reciprocating with aggressive acts' (1990: 78). By failing to acknowledge the male's view and by working from a model of victimization based primarily on women's experiences, counselors could increase the male survivor's sense of isolation and alienation.

Abuse by females

Little is known about abuse of both males and females by female offenders. Some authors (e.g. Kasl, 1990) have suggested that the prevalence of childhood sexual abuse by female offenders is higher than originally believed. Finkelhor and Russell (1984), for example, estimated that approximately 24 percent of male victims and 13 percent of female victims are abused by females. Often, these females were acting in conjunction with another offender. Under-reporting of abuse by females, especially in intra-familial situations, might be due to society's tendency to view males as aggressors and females as victims or due to possible differences in the types of offense committed by female offenders. Offenses by female offenders may be less overt and embedded in typical parenting behaviors and therefore not initially considered sexual abuse (e.g. caressing the child while bathing him or her, becoming sexual with a child while 'cuddling' in bed).

Because so little is known about abuse by female offenders it is premature to identify any specific counseling needs of survivors. However, it is believed that, in many situations, abuse by females is male-coerced and often accompanied by sexual and emotional abuse by both parents (Matthews et al., 1990). It is likely that the counseling needs of these survivors are quite complex.

Another scenario of abuse by females involves the extra-familial abuse of a younger male by an older woman, such as that between teacher and student. Often, each party considers this to be a 'love affair.' Due to cultural prescriptions, the male might not consider his experience abusive, but may experience long-term effects that he does not understand. Seemingly denial would be a significant counseling issue in this instance.

Structure of book

This book will discuss the counseling of adult survivors of childhood sexual abuse by identifying significant healing processes thought to be necessary for recovery. These processes include disclosing the abuse, focusing on the abuse experience, reinterpreting the abuse from an adult perspective, addressing issues related to the context of the abuse, making desired life changes, and dealing with abuse resolution issues. As each of these processes is discussed, counseling interventions that facilitate resolution will be addressed.

The individual counseling relationship will be emphasized, although a chapter will be devoted to group counseling. The book will discuss issues and interventions which are applicable to varied types of childhood sexual abuse (e.g. same-sex and opposite-sex abuse, abuse of males and females), although an effort will be made to avoid the assumption of 'universality' (Sepler, 1990) by addressing significant differences between abuse experiences when applicable.

Different specific relationship combinations of offenders and survivors (e.g. father–daughter, brother–sister, stranger–child) will not be addressed separately as it is believed that while the impact of the relationship between the victim and the offender is significant, relationship variables are complex and are influenced not just by the formal relationship between the two but by other factors, including emotional closeness or the amount of authority possessed by the offender. It is the overall closeness of the relationship, conceptualized on a continuum, that seems to have an impact on the survivor's perceptions of the psychological experience of the abuse, so this is considered more important than each specific relationship combination. However, as most survivors who seek treatment as adults are dealing with abuse that occurred in the context of their intimate social world, this will be the primary focus of the book.

Case examples will be given throughout. In most instances examples given are based on the author's clinical and research experiences with survivors and interventions described were utilized in her clinical practice. To ensure anonymity of individual clients and research participants, all names are changed and identifying facts are disguised. Some clinical examples are actually composites of several cases to protect the identity of specific individuals.

When the client referred to is now an adult who was abused as a child, the term 'survivor' will be used to avoid the connotations associated with the label of victim. When the client referred to is a child who is experiencing abuse, the term victim will be used to emphasize his or her inability to consent to the sexual activity. In all cases, clients in counseling who are dealing with having been sexually abused as children are considered individuals who have shared a common traumatic experience but who have unique needs, desires, and strengths.

2

Disclosing an Experience of Childhood Sexual Abuse

One of the initial tasks of the counselor working with adult survivors of childhood sexual abuse is to facilitate disclosure of their abusive experiences. Although many survivors today seek counseling to deal with their abuse issues and are prepared to disclose them, many individuals seek counseling for other concerns and do not reveal past childhood experiences with sexual abuse. This occurs for several reasons. In some cases, survivors may recall the abuse experience and recognize the significance it has played in their lives, but choose not to share it when initially meeting the counselor because they do not yet trust the counselor or feel 'ready' to disclose their experience.

Frequently, however, lack of disclosure in counseling is often related to the processes of 'protective denial' (Sgroi, 1989a). These processes include defensive mechanisms, which survivors used at the time of the abuse to protect themselves from emotional distress and which then become habitual coping mechanisms often used throughout the life span. For example, clients have often repressed some or all memories of their sexual abuse experiences. Such memory gaps are considered dissociative processes used to cope with traumatic experiences. Often memories may begin to return, sometimes as flashbacks or nightmares, after the survivor experiences a life event that triggers the repressed memories. These events could be developmental events that are symbolically related to the abuse (e.g. marriage, the birth of a child), a family crisis (e.g. the death of the offender), or actual or vicarious victimization experiences (e.g. the burglary of one's home). Survivors may seek help at this time because the returning memories are disturbing and perhaps inexplicable.

Some survivors may not have repressed memories of the abuse, but will deny the importance of the role that it has played in their lives, dissociate the affect connected with the abuse from the memories of the abuse, or deny that the sexual activity was abusive in nature. These survivors will often claim that they did not reveal the abuse in counseling initially because they believed it was 'in the past' or 'no big deal.' Such minimization may be especially pronounced in male victims as gender socialization often inhibits males from viewing themselves as victims.

This chapter will discuss the process of disclosure of a sexual abuse history within the counseling relationship. The counselor must often first detect a history of possible abuse based on the symptoms or issues that are presented by the client. Common presenting symptoms of survivors are listed and several models that organize these numerous and varied symptoms into conceptual frameworks are discussed. Techniques for assessing a history of abuse and helpful counselor responses to disclosure are outlined. Finally a case example of a survivor with a disguised presentation of incest is discussed.

Detecting a history of undisclosed incest

Common presenting symptoms
Survivors who do not initially disclose a history of childhood sexual abuse will often present with a variety of non-specific psychiatric symptoms or with various social or personal issues. Typically, survivors hope counseling will provide relief from these symptoms or difficulties. They may focus on one or two symptoms or may be troubled by many. Some of the more common presenting issues of survivors include:

Depressive symptoms including feelings of guilt and shame, low self-esteem, low self-efficacy, and unresolved grief.

Anxiety symptoms including generalized anxiety, phobias, panic attacks, trauma symptomatology (e.g. nightmares, flashbacks, dissociative experiences), and fear of invasive medical procedures.

Sexual problems including sexual dysfunction (e.g. impaired arousal, orgasmic difficulties, vaginismus, painful intercourse, impotence), avoidance of sexual intimacy, sexually aggressive and compulsive behaviors, sexual identity confusion, and general sexual dissatisfaction.

Interpersonal problems including difficulty forming and maintaining intimate relationships, a pattern of involvement in unsatisfactory relationships (sometimes involving continued physical, emotional, or sexual abuse), distrust of men or women, isolation, poor social skills, and parenting problems.

Self-destructive behaviors including substance abuse, eating disorders, self-mutilation, suicide attempts, and self-defeating behaviors (e.g. occupational underachievement, inability to provide enjoyable or relaxing activities for self).

Perceptual disturbances including visual (e.g. seeing 'shadowy' figures), auditory (e.g. hearing footsteps at night), and tactile (e.g. being touched by another) sensations.

Somatic complaints including pelvic pain, migraine headaches, and chronic sleep disturbances.

Aggressive behaviors including sexual offending, physical abuse of others, and antisocial conduct.

Models that organize presenting symptoms
Although the presence of several of these commonly experienced symptoms might suggest that the client has had some experience with childhood sexual abuse, these symptoms are numerous, varied, and non-specific, having many possible etiologies. Such lists can have only limited utility in detecting a history of undisclosed childhood sexual abuse. However, some authors have organized these symptoms into meaningful, conceptually-based frameworks to aid counselors in detecting an undisclosed history of sexual abuse and in understanding how these multiple and varied symptoms might be related to abusive experiences in childhood.

A predictive syndrome Ellenson, noting the wide variety of symptoms experienced by incest survivors, attempted to specify a 'syndrome that is exclusively related to a history of childhood incest' (1985: 525). He called this a predictive syndrome because he believed that the presence of certain characteristic symptoms could differentiate women who had been incestuously abused from those who had not. The framework is divided into symptoms reflecting thought content disturbances and perceptual disturbances. Certain combinations of the symptoms (e.g. seven total symptoms, five symptoms including at least one perceptual symptom) are thought to be highly predictive of incest, as these symptoms differ from symptoms that constitute other related syndromes (e.g. post-traumatic stress disorder (PTSD) resulting from a catastrophic event experienced in adulthood).

The recurring *thought* disturbances identified by Ellenson (1985) as characteristic of incest and the specific content of these disturbances are as follows:

1 Nightmares
   (a) catastrophes affecting oneself or one's family;
   (b) harm or death of children;
   (c) oneself or one's family being chased;
   (d) death or violent scenes.
2 Intrusive obsessions
   (a) impulses to hurt one's child;
   (b) feeling one's child is endangered.
3 Dissociative sensations
   (a) one's child is a stranger;
   (b) one's past is that of a stranger.
4 Persistent phobias
   (a) being alone;
   (b) being in physically compromising situations.

The recurring characteristic *perceptual* disturbances identified by Ellenson (1985) and the form these disturbances take are as follows:

1 Illusions
   (a) an evil entity is in the home;
   (b) an evil entity enters the self.
2 Auditory hallucinations
   (a) a person calling to the self;
   (b) intruder sounds (e.g. footsteps, doors opening);
   (c) 'booming' sounds.
3 Visual hallucinations
   (a) movement of objects or persons in one's peripheral vision;
   (b) shadowy figures;
   (c) appearance of dark figures at the bedside.
4 Tactile hallucinations
   (a) one's body being touched;
   (b) being pushed or thrown down.

Disguised presentation of undisclosed incest Gelinas has organized the varied and commonly reported symptoms of incest survivors into a 'coherent, explanatory, and heuristic framework' (1983: 312). She identifies three underlying negative effects: chronic, traumatic neurosis, continued relationship imbalances, and increased intergenerational risk of incest.

The intense affect and vivid memories experienced by survivors following disclosure and discussion of the incest are referred to as *chronic traumatic neurosis*. Phases of denial or repression alternate with intrusive experiences of trauma repetition (e.g. nightmares, pseudo-hallucinations, obsessions, emotional repetitions, behavioral re-enactments). Symptoms such as depression, anxiety, and substance abuse are secondary elaborations related to the hidden and untreated traumatic neurosis.

The *relational imbalances* exhibited by survivors are considered to be a result of the family dynamics that produced and maintained the secret of the incest. Gelinas (1983) discussed a scenario that typifies the development of incestuous family dynamics.

Parentification occurs when a child, often an eldest daughter, assumes responsibility for parental functions. The child learns to protect and nurture her parents, thereby developing a caretaking identity. She becomes skillful in meeting the needs of others but denies her own needs.

She chooses as a partner a man who requires caretaking, typically one who is needy, narcissistic, or insecure. As she might still be meeting the needs of her family of origin as well, she soon becomes emotionally depleted. When she and her husband have children, maternal caretaking is added to her responsibilities. She is then less able to attend to her husband's needs and might attempt to enlist his support. He feels both threatened and abandoned and becomes increasingly unavailable to her. She might then attempt to get emotional support from her child, often her eldest daughter, and this daughter then begins to experience parentification. The husband, if unable to meet his needs outside the family, may do so through his daughter. Sexual abuse is most likely to occur if the father is narcissistic, exhibits poor impulse control, and uses alcohol.

The daughter, now an incest survivor, becomes an adult who is also very skillful at caretaking, but who has a poor self-concept and is lacking the social skills needed to meet her own needs (e.g. assertiveness). She is unable to establish mutually supportive relationships with others and becomes isolated or abused and exploited in the relationships she does establish. As she also remains emotionally depleted, she will experience parenting difficulties and another generation of parentification may begin.

The *intergenerational risk* of incest is due to the establishment of the relationship imbalances discussed above. The incest survivor's daughter becomes at risk for incest as the processes of parentification and marital estrangement are repeated. The survivor, experiencing an untreated traumatic neurosis, will avoid stimuli that provoke memories of her own abuse and is therefore less likely to detect or attend to the sexual abuse of her daughter. Gelinas (1983) stressed that this does not suggest that the mother is to blame for the incest. Although each parent is responsible for the incestuous family dynamics, the offender alone is responsible for the sexual contact.

A framework for male survivors   Both the Gelinas (1983) and the Ellenson (1985) frameworks were proposed specifically for female survivors. At present there are no comprehensive frameworks which organize the long-term effects of males to suggest a disguised presentation of a history of childhood sexual abuse. However, Struve (1990) has identified nine factors, which he suggests have an impact on the recovery of male survivors, that might well serve as a basis of a framework to identify the disguised presentation of the male survivor. These nine factors are:

1 reluctance to seek treatment due to the beliefs that men are not victims and, if they are, that they are less traumatized by the victimizing experience than are females;
2 minimization of the experience of victimization due to the belief that sexual activity with an older woman is a privilege and that victimization by a male results from one's own sexual orientation;
3 shame-based personality dynamics based on one's perceived failure to protect oneself or to achieve appropriate revenge against the offender;
4 exaggerated efforts to reassert masculine identity in an attempt to compensate for the failure to protect oneself;
5 difficulties with male identity resulting in the avoidance of any behaviors perceived as feminine, including emotional intimacy with other males;
6 confusion about sexual identity due to one's perceived passivity or sexual arousal experienced during same-sex abuse;
7 behavior patterns with power/control dynamics due to attempts to overcompensate for the powerlessness experienced during the abuse.
8 externalization of feelings due to social prescriptions that males can act on, but not exprcss, their feelings;
9 vulnerability to compulsive behaviors due to attempts to deny feelings by excessive involvement with 'product- and task-orientated activities' (Struve, 1990: 38).

So male survivors may be even more likely than females to avoid treatment or disclosure and to minimize their abuse experience and will often present with behavioral (e.g. negative consequences of aggression), rather than emotionally expressive (e.g. complaints of depression), issues. A 'disguised' presentation may include exaggerated masculine or 'macho' behaviors, difficulties with intimacy

'As a child, were you ever touched in a way that felt uncomfortable (embarrassing, frightening) to you?'
'As a child, did anyone ever ask you to do something sexual that you did not like?'
'As a child, did anyone hurt you or use you in a sexual way?'

These questions, when coupled with a more traditional psychosexual history (e.g. 'Tell me about your first sexual experience'; 'How did you learn about sex?'), will often reveal a history of childhood sexual abuse. It is helpful to focus on the survivor's retrospective view of sexual events to determine if these events were experienced as exploitative although not labeled as such by the client. For example, in addition to asking when the client's first sexual experience occurred, it is helpful to ask how he or she *felt* about this and subsequent childhood sexual experiences.

Josephson and Fong-Beyette (1987) have researched factors that assist female clients' disclosure of incest in counseling. The authors interviewed thirty-seven women incest survivors who had been to a counselor and reported that those survivors who had disclosed their sexual abuse to their counselor indicated that they did so because they believed that they would feel better, because either a media piece or others encouraged them to do so, or because their counselors had directly inquired about the incest. Those who did not disclose their sexual abuse to their counselor reported that they were not thinking about the incest, did not believe it was related to their present concerns, or considered their present concerns to be more important. In addition, they reported that their counselors did not ask about their incest experiences. These authors recommend that counselors can elicit disclosure by directly questioning clients about childhood sexual abuse, as well as about emotional and physical abuse, along with more general questioning related to the quality of childhood experiences and family relationships (i.e. the client's best and worst childhood experiences). A structured assessment device to obtain a complete sexual history can also be used.

As well as indicating the possible presence of undisclosed abuse, the frameworks discussed above provide guidelines for determining what additional questions might be included in a sexual abuse inquiry. Ellenson (1985), for example, recommended a structured mental status exam related to the specific thought and perceptual disturbances that constitute the predictive syndrome (see pp. 19–20). Survivors may be concerned that these disturbances 'sound crazy', so may not reveal them unless asked specifically. The counselor should ask about the least unusual disturbances (e.g.

phobias) before asking about the more threatening symptoms (e.g. hallucinations). Ellenson also recommended that the counselor move from open-ended questions to specific questions, including asking for examples of experienced phenomena. It is important to inquire about the content of the disturbances experienced, as it is the content of the symptoms that is believed to be unique to incest survivors. For example, the counselor should not just ask if the client is having nightmares, but should ask what actually occurred in the nightmares.

Assessment questions based on Ellenson's (1988) framework could include:

1   Questions to address *thought disturbances:*
 'Do you have nightmares?'
 'Tell me what happens in your nightmares.'
 'Do the nightmares ever involve (a) catastrophes involving you and your family; (b) children being harmed; (c) chase scenes; (d) death scenes?'
 'Are you bothered by thoughts you feel you cannot control?'
 'What are these thoughts?'
 'Do your thoughts ever involve (a) hurting your child; (b) feeling your child is in some sort of danger?'
 'Do you have experiences that do not seem real to you?'
 'Tell me about these experiences.'
 'Do these experiences involve the feeling that (a) one's child is a stranger; (b) your past belongs to someone else?'
 'Are there things you are constantly afraid of?'
 'What are these things?'
 'Are you afraid of (a) being alone; (b) being in places you cannot escape from?'
2   Questions to address *perceptual disturbances:*
 'Do you ever feel the presence of things or persons that you know are not really there?'
 'Tell me about these feelings.'
 'Do you ever feel (a) the presence of something evil in your home; (b) the presence of something evil entering your body?'
 'Do you ever hear things that you suspect others do not?'
 'What are these things?'
 'Do you ever hear (a) a person calling you; (b) sounds of someone entering your home, room, etc. – such as footsteps?'
 'Do you ever see things that you suspect others do not?'
 'What are these things?'

'Do you ever see (a) things move in the corner of your eye; (b) shadowy figures when you are alone, in bed, etc?'
'Do you ever experience bodily sensations that feel strange or unreal?'
'Tell me about these sensations.'
'Do you sense that (a) your body is being touched; (b) someone is pushing you?'

Based on her hypothesis that the 'usual disguised presentation of the undisclosed victim is a characterological depression with complications and with atypical impulsive and dissociative elements' (1983: 326), Gelinas has proposed an 'Incest Recognition Profile', on which an assessment interview can be based. The profile includes a presenting problem of chronic depression with complications that stem from the affective disorder (e.g. substance abuse, suicidality), atypical dissociative elements (e.g. nightmares, depersonalization) and impulsive elements (e.g. impulsive eating, drinking, spending; child abuse), and a history of parentification (e.g. premature responsibilities in childhood). Gelinas considers a 'complaint of confusion in a non-psychotic person' (1983: 327) the best single indicator of an undisclosed history of incest. Assessment of undisclosed incest should include questions related not only to the presenting problem but also to the atypical elements and a history of parentification as well.

In addition to questions used to assess the presenting problem, an assessment based on Gelinas' (1983) framework could also include:

1 Questions to address the *atypical, dissociative elements:*
'Do you often feel easily confused?'
'Do you frequently experience nightmares?' [If yes]: 'Tell me about them.'
'Do you experience distressing reactions to certain people or events?' [If yes]: 'Tell me about these reactions.'
'Do you have experiences that do not seem real?' [If yes]: 'Tell me about them.'
'Do you ever feel as if you are separate from your body?' [If yes]: 'Tell me how.'
'Do you ever "blank out"?'
2 Questions to address the *atypical, impulsive elements:*
'Do you do things that you regret afterward?' [If yes]: 'Tell me about some of them.'
'Do you sometimes feel that you cannot control your behavior?'
'Do you have problems with (a) overeating; (b) drinking or

using drugs; (c) overspending; (d) sexual activities; (e) frequent accidents; (f) hurting your children?'
3 Questions to address a history of *parentification:*
   'Tell me what your responsibilities were in your family when you were a child.'
   'Do you feel that you grew up too quickly?'
   'How did you help your mom, your dad?'
   'Are there things you feel you missed out on when you were a child?'
   'As a child, how did you have fun?'

Struve's (1990) work might be utilized as a guideline to select questions for males whom the counselor suspects may have experienced sexual abuse. These questions should be asked from a male 'perspective.' As the male survivor may not conceptualize his experience as abusive or victimizing, he may resist being asked if he were a 'victim' of sexual 'abuse.' Rather, the counselor might first ask him if he had a sexual experience with an older woman or with another male as a child and then ask for his perceptions of these experiences. Questions asked of suspected male survivors should initially focus on behaviors rather than on feelings. Assessment of male survivors needs to address not only the self-destructive behaviors that are often the focus of interviews with women but aggressive and compulsive behaviors as well.

In addition to questions related to specific perceptual disturbances and dissociative experiences, questions to assess the presence of sexual abuse in the histories of male survivors might include the following:

'As a child, did you ever have a sexual experience with a female who was older than yourself?' [If yes]: 'What was the experience like for you?'
'As a child, did you ever have a sexual experience with a male?' [If yes]: 'What was this experience like for you?'
'Did anyone do anything to you as a child that you would like to get back at them for?'
'How do you handle things now when someone wrongs you?'
'Are there things you do now that you would like to stop doing or things that cause trouble for you relating to (a) sexual behaviors; (b) drinking or drug use; (c) eating; (d) working too much; (e) fighting?'

Detecting a history of undisclosed childhood sexual abuse therefore involves first and foremost the use of sensitive and direct questions about abusive childhood experiences using phrasing that has meaning to the client. These questions should be accompanied by general questions related to early sexual experiences and family dynamics. Questions assessing symptoms thought to be related specifically to sexual abuse experience, such as Ellenson's (1985) predictive syndrome, Gelinas' (1983) atypical elements, or Struve's (1990) nine factors related to male survivors, should be included. Finally, questions related specifically to incestuous family dynamics, such as the process of parentification, should be part of the assessment.

Counselor's responses during the disclosure process

Immediate responses to disclosure

The counselor's initial response to the client's disclosure of childhood sexual abuse is extremely important. Disclosure, if not handled skillfully by the counselor, can have deleterious effects. If survivors perceive the counselor's response to disclosure to be non-supportive, they may leave counseling, resist further discussion of the abuse issue, or minimize the impact of their abuse experience (Josephson and Fong-Beyette, 1987). Not believing clients who reveal a history of childhood abuse, blaming them for the abuse, asking intrusive or voyeuristic questions related to the abuse, or minimizing the importance of the abuse are examples of non-supportive responses.

In a qualitative study of the healing process of incest survivors (Draucker, 1992), several participants reported that one of the most destructive counselor responses to disclosure is that of shock, termed by the survivors as 'Oh, my God' or 'Jaw drop' responses. Although counselors may perceive such intense reactions to be empathic or genuine given the survivor's 'horrible' stories, survivors believe these responses confirm their feelings of stigma and isolation. One survivor in this study, for example, stated:

> A lot of what happens for an incest survivor is very threatening to people who haven't been through it, and any kind of disbelief or shock or 'Oh, my God' you know, that kind of judgement is very damaging to me. One of the things that my first counselor did at our first meeting was she just, her mouth dropped open and she just said, 'Oh, my God!' and I have just been telling her the basic things in my life.

Counselors who reacted calmly but with 'appropriate concern' were perceived by survivors to be both empathic and yet 'strong enough' to deal with the abuse issues.

Other helpful counselor responses following disclosure include congratulating the survivor for taking the difficult step of disclosing, offering support and indicating one's availability after the session during which the client disclosed, inviting the survivor to discuss the abuse at his or her own pace (Hall and Lloyd, 1989), and evaluating the client's mental status and determining any immediate safety concerns (e.g. suicidal thoughts).

Examples of non-helpful responses:

'Oh, my God. I can't believe anyone could actually do anything that horrible to a child. What your father did was disgusting.' (shock response)

'It sounds like you *believe* your father did these things to you. You were so young, it is hard to know what really happened.' (disbelief)

'*Why* did you agree to have sex with him? *Why* did you not tell your mother? *Why* did it go on for so long?' (blaming)

'You say that this experience is in the past and that you've coped with it. Why don't we move on then to the concerns you have today?' (minimization)

'Tell me exactly what he did to you sexually.' (voyeuristic response)

Examples of helpful counselor responses:

'I am concerned about the experience you shared with me and would like to hear more about it. Sexual abuse can be a very painful experience for children and can continue to have an impact on one's life as an adult.' (showing calm concern without showing disgust)

'I can imagine it was hard for you to share that experience with me. I respect your courage for being able to do so.' (acknowledging difficulty of disclosure)

'It can be very important to discuss your sexual abuse experience as so often it is related to your current concerns. However, we can do this at a pace that feels right to you.' (reinforcing client's control of disclosure process)

'For some women (men), sharing an abuse experience for the first time (with a counselor) can result in some very strong (confusing, distressing) feelings. How are you feeling now? . . . Do you feel unsafe in any way?' (acknowledging feelings, assessing safety)

Responses to clients who do not disclose abuse

Some survivors may choose not to disclose an experience of abuse even when asked and, in some instances, defensive processes remain strong and repression continues even after inquiry. If the counselor strongly suspects a history of childhood sexual abuse, based on presenting symptomatology, and the client does not disclose this experience upon inquiry, the counselor may 'gently confront' (Josephson and Fong-Beyette, 1987: 478) the client by suggesting that his or her symptoms are frequently experienced by someone who has been abused at some point in childhood. Defining incest or sexual abuse may stimulate clients to explore their early sexual experiences, even if they had not previously considered them 'abusive.' This may be especially important for male survivors. The counselor might also discuss the benefits of disclosing an abusive experience, while acknowledging the pain involved (Hall and Lloyd, 1989).

However, while counselors should provide opportunities and support for disclosure, they must always respect survivors' right not to disclose or their inability to remember an abusive experience even when the counselor strongly suspects that abuse occurred. There is always the possibility that a client without a history of abuse may have a presentation that closely resembles that of a survivor. Counselors may 'leave the door open,' but should never pressure or manipulate a client to obtain a disclosure.

Possible counselor responses to clients who do not disclose a history of abuse, but whom the counselor strongly suspects may have suffered abuse, may include the following:

'The symptoms and concerns you describe are often experienced by women (men) who have experienced sexual abuse as a child even though they may not remember the experience because it was so painful. If, as we go along, you suspect something like that might have happened to you, it would be helpful for us to talk about it, even though it can be very difficult to discuss.' (suggestion that client's symptoms are typical of sexual abuse, acknowledging possible repression of memories, leaving the door open to discuss abuse)

'Sometimes women (men) have had sexual experiences in childhood that they do not consider sexual abuse, but which may nevertheless have been hurtful to them. When I speak of sexual abuse, I refer to any incidents in which a child was used sexually to meet the needs of an older or more powerful person. The sexual activity does not have to involve intercourse. It could include, for example, any touching that made the child feel uncomfortable or frightened.' (defining sexual abuse)

Counselor responses to minimization
Because many survivors disclose the abuse but continue to minimize the impact it has had on their lives, an initial response that acknowledges and validates the significance of the sexual abuse and suggests that the abuse may be related to survivors' current difficulties is important (Josephson and Fong-Beyette, 1987). (Because minimization often continues to be an important issue long after the initial disclosure, it is discussed further in the next chapter.) One participant in the incest healing study (Draucker, 1992), when asked what counselors could do to facilitate the healing of survivors, stated that counselors should assume, at least initially, that survivors have 'scars' rather than accept that the abuse was not significant because a survivor gives it 'proper lip service.' Counselors should validate the possible impact of the abuse, give the survivor a choice related to further exploration, and indicate that the counselor will 'be with' the survivor during such exploration.

Possible counselor responses to a client who is minimizing the abuse include the following:

'In my work with clients, I've learned that an experience such as you describe can have an impact on individuals in ways they might not be aware of. Would you be willing to explore this with me further?'

'The childhood experience you tell me about can have something to do with your current distress. May we discuss how that experience might be connected to your current pain?'

Disclosures of false or created abuse experiences
Often, when an in-depth assessment of a particular clinical issue, such as a history of sexual abuse, is recommended, counselors express concern that the inquiry itself may 'plant' a suggestion that an experience occurred when in fact it did not, and a client will therefore 'create' a memory of sexual abuse. A related concern is that an in-depth assessment of a history of sexual abuse will result in clients falsely disclosing abuse experiences for secondary gain (e.g. the counselor's attention), to please the counselor, or as a result of psychotic thinking.

Although undoubtedly some clients may give false disclosures or construct abuse memories as a way of explaining their current distress, these occurrences are considered rare (Briere, 1989). Herman addressed this issue in a discussion of counselor reluctance to assess for a history of childhood sexual abuse:

The therapists' wish to shy away from the possibility of incest is often disguised as concern for the patient. They may express the fear that direct questioning will offend or frighten the patient or 'put ideas into her head.' Such solicitude is rarely necessary. A woman who is not troubled by a history of incest will simply answer no and go on to talk about things that bother her. (1981: 178)

Similarly, Briere addressed concern about the emphasis many counselors place on determining whether sexual abuse disclosures reflect what 'really happened' in the client's life.

More basically, the therapist must question herself as to why the 'real facts' are so important in treating adults who report childhood molestation. In other areas of psychotherapy, it is often benignly assumed the clients' reports of past events – although frequently distorted by defenses and previous experiences – are essentially true, and the client is rarely cross-examined as to the detailed aspects of her historical account. Nevertheless, some therapists appear to be significantly invested in determining absolute truth or falsehood when the client issue is sexual victimization. (1989: 53)

Typically, it is preferable for counselors to risk the limited chance that a client will falsely disclose abuse in response to an in-depth evaluation rather than avoid a thorough assessment. Also, counselor behaviors can decrease the risk of constructed memories or false disclosures. Clients should never be 'persuaded' to disclose a history of abuse (Hall and Lloyd, 1989) and counselors should always ask assessment questions in a calm, matter-of-fact manner, never suggesting that an abuse history is what they 'want to hear.' When clients initially deny or are unable to recall abusive experiences, follow-up questions should be asked in a tentative manner (e.g.: '*Some* women who experience flashbacks such as the ones you describe have experienced sexual abuse as a child. *Could* you have had such an experience at some time?')

Case example

The following case description exemplifies a disguised presentation of childhood sexual abuse and the process of the initial disclosure in counseling. Jean, a 34-year-old woman, was seen in a mental health center following a family crisis in which her husband, Jack, aged 42, was charged with physically abusing the couple's 16-year-old son, Bill. The couple also had another son, Tom, aged 14, and a daughter, Sally, aged 12. A family session revealed that Jack had beaten Bill following an altercation regarding Bill's desire to leave school. The incident closely followed Jack's being fired from his job after a disagreement with his boss. Some bruises on Bill's arm were noticed by a teacher and reported to the child protective agency who referred the family for counseling.

A family assessment revealed that Jack frequently used physical discipline (i.e. spanking) on his sons, although Bill and Jean both reported that the recent beating was the most 'serious.' The abuse typically occurred when Jack had been drinking. Physical abuse of Sally was denied by all family members, who claimed that Sally was a 'good girl' who never did anything wrong.

Jean was referred for individual therapy following the family assessment as she had revealed some vague suicidal ideation during the course of the meeting. She claimed that she was 'too tired' to deal with any more family problems, especially the fighting between Jack and Bill, and wished she 'never had to get out of bed again.'

An individual session revealed that Jean was the oldest of eight children in her family. She reported that her father was an alcoholic with a 'mean' temper who had worked at a local factory until his death several years previously. He was physically abusive of his sons but never hit Jean, who was always 'well behaved.' She described her mother as being a kind and gentle woman who was always sickly but who 'waited on my father hand and foot.'

Jean reported that she married Jack when she was 17 because she saw marriage as a way of escaping her extensive responsibilities of caring for the younger children in the family. Also, Jack was 'pushing' her to marry shortly after high school graduation. Soon after they were married, Bill was born. Jean described the first year of Bill's life as a happy time for her. However, when she become pregnant with Tom, Jack began drinking heavily and would sometimes 'shove her around.' She explained that her husband demanded much of her attention. The drinking continued over the years but Jack's abuse of her subsided. Jean stated that she never enjoyed their sexual life and eventually tried to avoid sex, although Jack would often demand it when he had been drinking. Jean revealed that she had 'given up' on the boys. She would attempt to discipline them in a non-physical manner (e.g. by 'grounding them'), but they would never listen to her. Although Jean stated she was not close to either boy, she indicated that she was very close to Sally. She and Sally would often go shopping together and Sally would listen to her problems. Jean worked as a sales clerk at a local mall. She had started working on a college degree at a local community college on several occasions but stopped because of 'family responsibilities.'

Shortly after Sally was born, Jean went to a psychiatrist and was treated for 'post-partum depression.' She was given an antidepressant drug at that time. Records revealed that Jack and Jean had been to the clinic for marriage counseling several years prior to the current crisis. A school guidance counselor had recommended they seek help after Bill had gotten into several scraps with the law for petty theft and Tom, at age 11, had failed the fifth grade. It was recommended at that time that Jack attend Alcoholics Anonymous. Jean was diagnosed as having a dysthymic (i.e. depressive) disorder and a dependent personality disorder. The couple discontinued counseling after three sessions. Jean then saw the counselor individually on several occasions. These sessions focused on her troubled marriage and on the behavioral problems of her sons.

Jean told her current counselor that she was feeling depressed and admitted to feeling 'somewhat' suicidal at times. She said that she was spending most of the morning in bed. When the current crisis of Bill's beating occurred, she considered taking an overdose of some of her mother's 'nerve' pills but was 'too chicken' to do so. She stated she had lost over 10 pounds in two weeks. She denied any substance abuse herself. Her main complaint was that 'I'm just tired of it all and I want some peace.'

Assessment of Jean's presenting problem and history revealed that she exhibited several of the long-term effects frequently seen in adult survivors of abuse, including depression; low self-esteem and self-efficacy; general sexual dissatisfaction; an unsatisfactory marital relationship involving physical abuse and the alcoholism of her husband; and parenting difficulties. Her symptom pattern was somewhat consistent with Gelinas' (1983) 'Incest Recognition Profile' as Jean did exhibit chronic depression with 'complications' (e.g. sexual dissatisfaction, interpersonal difficulties). Her history of parentification was also clear. As the oldest child of a family of eight children she had assumed many of her mother's responsibilities, as her mother was viewed as weak and sickly. Her father was a dependent, needy man who abused alcohol. Jean married a man who was also needy and immature and who needed caretaking. Jean was unable to meet her own needs and began to show symptoms of depression after the birth of her third child, although she agreed she was 'worn out' long before that time. Although there was no evidence that her daughter Sally had been sexually abused, Sally was experiencing parentification. At the age of 12 she had assumed the role of the responsible child and had begun to be her mother's confidante.

Because of her background and presenting symptoms, an assessment of a history of abuse was indicated. Jean probably would not have revealed her abuse experiences to the counselor unless directly asked. The following dialogue reflects the interaction between Jean and the counselor that led to the disclosure of sexual abuse by

Jean's father. The disclosure occurred when the counselor was inquiring about Jean's childhood experiences and followed Jean's denial that she had been physically abused by her father as her brothers had been.

> *Counselor:* You describe some difficult times in your childhood. Did anyone hurt you or use you in a sexual way?
>
> *Jean:* Well, yes, I guess you could say so. I really don't like to talk about it. It's kind of embarrassing. It was my father. I guess it doesn't matter much now.
>
> *Counselor:* I realize this can be difficult to talk about. Oftentimes, sexual experiences in childhood are hurtful and can continue to influence women as adults. Therefore, it could be helpful for us to discuss it further. Would you be willing to do so?
>
> *Jean:* Ya, I guess so. It happened so long ago, though. It wasn't like we really had sex or anything.
>
> *Counselor:* What did happen?
>
> *Jean:* It would usually happen when he was drunk, which was not all the time. Maybe once a month or so. He would come into my room and feel me up – mostly my breasts, sometimes my private parts. It happened mostly when I was in junior high. [*Jean begins to cry.*] He would sometimes pass out in my bed but he always found his way back to his own by morning. I was afraid my mother would find out. It would have killed her. He stopped when I started to get interested in boys, I think. I really can't talk more about this any more. It's really my Billy that I'm concerned about.
>
> *Counselor:* I really respect your courage for telling me about this. I can see that it has brought up painful memories for you. How you are feeling now?
>
> *Jean:* Weird. I've never talked about it before. I guess I figured it is best to leave it dead and buried. It is so embarrassing, you know. I don't know, I feel kind of sad. I'll be OK, though.
>
> *Counselor:* You may experience many different feelings after sharing this experience with me. Please feel free to contact me if you feel the need to talk about your feelings before we meet again. I also know you have been having some thoughts related to suicide . . . .
>
> *Jean:* Yes, but like I said, I won't do anything.
>
> *Counselor:* If the thoughts get stronger or if you feel unsafe in any way, will you call me?
>
> *Jean:* Yes. Will we talk about my father again next time? I don't think it will help with my problems with Jack or Bill, but I don't know.
>
> *Counselor:* Although it can be very difficult to deal with, I do recommend we discuss it further. However, it is up to you. Many of the things you are experiencing now, including your relationships with Bill and Tom, could be influenced by what happened with your father. We can explore how this could be so. We can go at a pace that feels right for you so that talking about this will not seem so overwhelming. We would focus on how the abuse relates to your current problems, as it is these problems that trouble you now.
>
> *Jean:* Maybe it is important. I've seen some movies about this kind of thing. I'll think some about it.

When the counselor inquired about sexual abuse, Jean disclosed a history of abuse by her father. She remembered having been abused over the course of several years but did not disclose the experience in past counseling situations, or in her most recent situation until asked directly, because it was 'embarrassing' and because she did not consider it a significant life experience. Although she had not repressed the memories of the experience, she did minimize the impact it had had on her life. The counselor initially intervened by acknowledging the difficulty of disclosure, validating the significance of the abuse, and inviting Jean to discuss it further.

Although the counselor did not probe for details, she did ask Jean to describe the experience. Jean explained that the abuse, lasting several years, involved her father fondling her breasts and genitals in her bed at night when he had been drinking. At this point Jean became tearful and indicated she did not want to continue discussing the abuse. Counseling interventions were aimed at acknowledging the courage it took for Jean to discuss this experience, exploring her feelings, assessing her safety needs, and stressing the counselor's availability. The counselor also proposed a connection between this experience and Jean's current concerns and suggested that they explore the issue further at a pace that Jean controlled.

3
Focusing on the Abuse Experience

Once clients have disclosed a history of childhood sexual abuse, the next phase of counseling is the focus on the sexual abuse experience. This includes several processes including addressing the minimization that often follows disclosure, establishing a sexual abuse contract, reviewing the sexual abuse experience, retrieving repressed memories, and dealing with possible client responses to the focus on sexual abuse. Each of these processes is discussed in this chapter.

Dealing with minimization following disclosure

Even after a history of childhood sexual abuse has been established, clients often continue to minimize the abuse experience or fail to connect it with their current concerns. If counselors do not encourage clients to explore the impact the abuse has had on their lives, the focus of counseling will remain on the presenting symptoms and the abuse issue will remain unresolved, even though it has been disclosed. Several of the participants who were interviewed for the incest healing study (Draucker, 1992) discussed having minimized their abuse experiences in order to survive. For these survivors coming to believe that the incest was a 'major problem,' that it 'cost' them, or that it had had a 'profound effect' on them was necessary for them to begin healing. One survivor, for example, discussed telling several counselors throughout the years that she had been sexually abused by her father but had put that experience behind her. Her counselors 'went along with' this assessment and the abuse was never addressed. She believed that she began to heal when her last therapist suggested that the abuse might have been a significant life experience and invited her to discuss it further. The survivor stated:

> She [the therapist] did make me recognize the fact that it was a big deal and just knowing it was a big deal made me concentrate more on it. I hadn't realized that – how big a deal it was. It was affecting every aspect of my life, not just my personal relationships, everything I did revolved around my problem with incest.

Survivors often call making a connection between their current distress and their history of abuse a 'clicking' experience. It is only when survivors accept that there are connections between their current experiences and their abuse experiences, although they may not yet understand what these connections are, that they will begin to explore the meaning their abuse experiences have had in their lives. When clients have trouble entertaining a connection between past experiences and present distress, counselors may give examples of how experiences of childhood sexual abuse can be related to problems in adulthood. The following counselor response, for example, can be used:

> Let me give you an example of how childhood abuse can affect one's life. Sometimes, individuals who were sexually abused as children by a parent may have trouble trusting others when they are adults because their parent, someone on whom they depended, violated their trust to the extent that they could not learn to trust others.

At this point, counselors may also introduce the idea that clients' present dysfunctional behaviors may have started out as adaptive mechanisms used to survive the abuse. The following is an example of this type of intervention:

> Although your inability to express your anger is now a problem, as a little girl, expressing anger toward your parents would have resulted in more hurt for you. Avoiding anger doesn't help you now but as a child it protected you.

Clients may then begin to view themselves as survivors as they develop an understanding of the cause of their current difficulties.

Struve (1990) has suggested that minimization is an especially salient issue for male survivors. As mentioned earlier, a sexual encounter with an older woman may be considered a 'rite of passage' and a childhood sexual encounter with an older male may be considered a reflection of the survivor's homosexuality. As Johanek states, 'A surprising number of adult male victims are themselves unaware of their own sexual abuse history. They are not in a state of repression but simply do not realize that some of the events that took place in childhood were sexual molestation' (1988: 111). Counselors should be sensitive to the process of minimization following disclosure in male survivors by cautiously exploring connections between their current issues and their childhood sexual experiences.

The sexual abuse contract

If a counselor has assessed that a client's problems are related to the long-term effects of sexual abuse, and the client has considered that the sexual abuse experience was important and that it may continue to interfere with his or her current functioning, the counselor may contract with the survivor to focus on the sexual abuse as a major treatment issue. The counselor may introduce a contract with a statement such as the following:

> It is very important that we address all of the concerns that brought you to counseling, but I do believe that these concerns are related in some way to the experiences you had as a child. Therefore, I recommend we explore the abuse and see how it relates to your current distress. That way, we won't just be putting a 'Band-aid' on the different problems you've been having but rather we'll try to understand what underlies these problems. This approach can be frightening but we can go at a pace that feels right to you. Are you interested in taking this approach to your counseling?

Setting a contract such as this with a survivor has several purposes. A contract gives the counseling a focus, something that has often been missing in the prior treatment of survivors, and also avoids separate counselor and client agendas regarding this focus. When the counselor makes a decision to focus on the abuse without stating this explicitly to the client and the client continues to expect symptomatic treatment, the counseling is often unsuccessful. Introducing the contract with a statement such as the above allows the counselor to acknowledge the importance of the client's current concerns and avoids the message that the abuse is important but the client's current distress is not.

A contract also emphasizes the client's choice to pursue this treatment approach. A 'rescuing' dynamic between counselor and client can thus be avoided with a contract. If the client as an adult agrees to pursue exploration of the abuse, he or she becomes an active participant who has chosen a painful course rather than a victim who is being 'rescued' by the counselor in ways that the client has not agreed to.

Ingram (1985), who discussed the treatment of adult survivors from a Gestalt perspective, suggested that the initial phase of treatment involves a figure–ground shift. A contract removes the abuse from the background, where it has been influencing the client in covert ways, to the forefront of treatment so that it can be openly examined. As Josephson and Fong-Beyette state, 'Clients should be encouraged to allow themselves to dwell on the incest in order to give attention and importance to an area that they or others in their environment may have tried to ignore or minimize' (1987: 478).

Reviewing the sexual abuse experience

Describing the abuse experience to the counselor
Following contracting, the counselor can encourage survivors to describe the circumstances of their childhood sexual abuse experience. Although voyeuristic or intrusive questions are to be avoided, most authors (Blake-White and Kline, 1985; Faria and Belohlavek, 1984; Joy, 1987; Tsai and Wagner, 1978) agree that a necessary component of the recovery process is the client's description of the details of their abuse to the counselor. Counselors should inquire about the following abuse factors:

- the duration and the frequency of the abuse;
- the client's relationship to the offender;
- methods used to carry out the offense (e.g. physical force, other methods of coercion);
- the type of sexual activity involved;
- the age of the child and the age of the offender at the time of the abuse.

Other important contextual factors should also be part of the inquiry:

- the role of other family members in the abuse;
- circumstances that altered the course of or ended the abuse;
- results of disclosure or of exposure (e.g. involvement of social service agencies or the criminal justice system);
- other important family issues (e.g. parental alcoholism, emotional or physical abuse within the family).

The description of the sexual abuse experience is important for two reasons. The counselor's awareness of the circumstances of the abuse situation is helpful because specific abuse characteristics can influence clients' perceptions of the role the abuse played in their lives and because certain characteristics may be related to specific long-term effects. Also, it is important for survivors to have the opportunity to describe their experience to a non-judgmental other as this process serves to validate the reality of the experience and allows them to begin to reintegrate the abuse experience in their lives.

Counselors should discuss the rationale for the process of the description of the abuse experience. Survivors often have had the experience of disclosing the abuse experience to others, only to have them respond with excessive questioning based on curiosity rather than concern. Survivors need to clearly understand that describing the abuse helps the counselor understand and appreciate what the survivors experienced as children.

Questions used to facilitate this process should be direct and specific, although counselors need to be sensitive to the fact that parts of the experience (e.g. the type of sexual activity involved) may be very difficult for survivors to discuss. As with other counseling processes discussed thus far, it is important that the descriptions of the abuse experience are paced according to the survivors' responses to this process and that survivors have control over this pacing.

A conceptual framework

Finkelhor and Browne have proposed a comprehensive model that outlines four trauma-producing factors, called traumagenic dynamics, in the sexual abuse situation. They state: 'These dynamics alter children's cognitive and emotional orientation to the world, and create trauma by distorting children's self-concept, world-view, and affective capacities' (1985: 531). Each of the four dynamics results from certain characteristics in the abuse situation and is related to certain long-term effects. The four dynamics are discussed below.

Traumatic sexualization results when characteristics in the abuse situation result in the development of children's sexuality in ways that are 'developmentally inappropriate and interpersonally dysfunctional' (1985: 531). For example, when rewards are given for sexual behaviors, when a particular part of a child's body is fetishized, when the child is given misleading information regarding sexuality, or when frightening memories become associated with sexual behaviors, traumatic sexualization occurs. This dynamic is associated with long-term effects such as precocious, aggressive, or indiscriminate sexual behaviors, sexual dysfunctions, sexual identity confusion, and sexual avoidance.

Betrayal results when children realize that an adult whom they trusted and depended on caused them harm. Betrayal can occur both when children realize they were exploited or 'taken in' by the offender and when they realize they were not protected or believed by other family members. The dynamic of betrayal is associated with long-term effects such as isolation, disturbed interpersonal relationships, further abuse, and aggression.

Powerlessness results when children's attempts to meet their needs are persistently frustrated or when they are threatened with injury or harm. Powerlessness results from invasion of the body, violence accompanying the sexual activity, or from children's inability to halt or alter the course of the abuse. This dynamic is associated with long-term effects such as trauma symptomatology (e.g. nightmares, flashbacks), low self-efficacy resulting in failure and underachievement, and compensatory behaviors such as aggression and delinquency.

Stigmatization occurs when children are told they are bad, shameful, or worthless and these messages are incorporated into their self-concept. These messages may be given by the offender at the time of the abuse or by significant others at the time of disclosure. Stigmatization can occur whenever children are blamed or punished for the sexual activity. Associated effects may include low self-esteem, guilt, and self-destructive behavior.

This model can guide counselors in determining what aspects of the abuse situation might be especially salient for the client so that the counselor may encourage thorough description of those aspects of the abuse. For example, if the client exhibits significant interpersonal problems, it might be especially important to discuss the circumstances related to the betrayal dynamic (e.g. the role of significant others). If the client seems to be overwhelmed with guilt, it might be essential to explore circumstances related to the stigmatization dynamic (e.g. messages of worthlessness). As the model is comprehensive in addressing multiple situational factors, counselors can use the model to determine what aspects of the abuse situation have not been addressed during the client's description of the abuse experience.

Case vignette
The following dialogue exemplifies questions that the counselor may ask to begin to elicit the client's description of the abuse experience. This client is a 23-year-old woman, Sarah, who was molested at the age of 10 by her stepfather.

> *Counselor:* Part of the work of dealing with a sexual abuse experience is describing what happened to you. By telling me what happened, I can better understand and appreciate your experience. Although describing your experience can be difficult, it can also help you to begin to make the experience seem more real and you can therefore begin to more fully understand the impact it had on you. Are you feeling ready to discuss the experience you had with your stepfather?
>
> *Sarah:* Yes, I guess so. Although I really do not remember the whole thing. I think it happened when my mother went into the hospital to have my sister. Bob came into my room and told me he was going to teach me something I was old enough to know. I told him I didn't want to, but my mother was always telling me he was my father now and I should do what he said.

Counselor: What did he do to you?

Sarah: He got into my bed and began kissing me. It was disgusting. When I told him I was going to tell my mother, he slapped me and told me she would not believe me. He was probably right. He told me to stop being such a sissy.

Counselor: So he not only kissed you, he hit you and insulted you as well. Did he do anything else to you?

Sarah: Yes, he made me rub his penis until he, you know, ejaculated.

Counselor: Do you remember how you felt then as a child?

Sarah: I was mostly disgusted. I hated him anyway. My mom was completely devoted to him. Still is. I don't think I was afraid, just sick to my stomach.

Counselor: Did the abuse happen again?

Sarah: Yes, a few more times while my mom was still in the hospital. She had some complications. One time he tried to have sex with me.

Counselor: Intercourse?

Sarah: Yes, I really freaked out. Started crying hysterically so he left me alone.

Counselor: How did the abuse stop?

Sarah: After that time. You know I think he was afraid I would tell my mother. He used to spank us kids a lot, but after that he never touched me. Kind of ignored me. Anyway, she came home from the hospital.

Counselor: Did anyone know what you had been through?

Sarah: No, not until now. I pretended it never happened.

The counselor facilitated description of the abuse experience by explaining why the description process is helpful while acknowledging that it can be difficult. The counselor then began to ask questions regarding the circumstances and context of the abuse (e.g. the type of sexual activity involved, the duration of the abuse, the client's recollection of her reaction as a child, the circumstances surrounding termination of the abuse, whether the abuse has been disclosed to others). More in-depth description of particular incidents may continue throughout counseling, often as more specific memories are retrieved.

Retrieving repressed memories

The review of the sexual abuse experience may be hindered for many survivors as some memories may remain repressed. These survivors may be certain, or may strongly suspect, that the abuse occurred but have little or no recall of the actual events. Other survivors report vague memories that do not seem real. Marked memory deficits typically occur in survivors whose abuse was characterized by early onset and violent or sadistic episodes (Herman and Schatzow, 1987).

Although retrieval of repressed memories can result in intense affective responses and trauma symptomatology, the process is considered necessary for recovery (Herman and Schatzow, 1987). Such retrieval allows survivors to understand experiences (e.g. reactions to 'trigger' events, disturbing dreams) that previously made little sense to them and to reintegrate the abuse into their life history in a meaningful way. Memory retrieval may also often result in eventual relief from post-traumatic stress symptomatology (Herman and Schatzow, 1987).

Counseling interventions
Techniques to precipitate memory retrieval or to confirm memories that do not seem real can be used in counseling. As with other processes that precipitate intense emotional responses, memory retrieval techniques should be paced, should be the survivor's choice, and should be accompanied by the support and reassurance of the counselor. When using any of these techniques, counselors may discuss with survivors what they hope to accomplish, what they imagine the experience will be like for them, how they might feel if the technique is not successful, and how they might handle their possible affective response to retrieval if it occurs. Counseling interventions that can be useful in memory retrieval include the following.

Clients are advised to bring to counseling sessions old family photographs, scrapbooks, diaries, and other memorabilia from the period that they believe the abuse occurred. The counselor and the client then focus on any memories that are evoked by viewing and discussing these materials.

In some instances, counselors may recommend that survivors return to the scene of the abuse to precipitate memory retrieval. Going back to one's home town and visiting the family home of one's childhood can be a powerful experience. Counselors discuss with the survivor any memories that were provoked by this visit. In some cases, counselors actually accompany survivors on these visits to provide support.

Counselors may facilitate the validation or retrieval of memories by suggesting that survivors contact family or friends who might have some knowledge of family functioning at the time of the abuse. Asking siblings about their childhood experiences, for example, and finding that they were also abused can result in retrieval of memories or confirmation of survivors' suspicions that they were abused. Sometimes, simply reminiscing with significant others from the past, without discussing the abuse *per se*, can provoke repressed memories.

In some instances, counselors may refer survivors to a specially trained hypnotist to uncover deeply repressed traumatic memories of the abuse (Faria and Belohlavek, 1984; Urbancic, 1987). The use of hypnosis with survivors is controversial as they may perceive hypnosis as a loss of control, a salient concern of most survivors. However, in some cases, hypnosis, conducted by a practitioner who is trained in working with abuse survivors and who uses naturalistic methods that allow survivors to control their own trance, can be successful (Malmo, 1990).

Clients may be referred to a survivors' group to aid in memory retrieval. The stimulation of hearing the abuse experiences of other survivors in a group situation is extremely effective in precipitating memory retrieval for survivors with partial repression of abuse experiences as well as for those who have complete amnesia (Herman and Schatzow, 1987). (The use of survivor groups as an adjunct to counseling will be discussed in detail later.)

Case vignette
The following dialogue exemplifies the utility of viewing old family photographs as a method of stimulating memory retrieval. The client, Janet, was a 36-year-old woman who strongly suspected that she had been abused by her older brother, John. She asked her grandmother for an old photo album that contained pictures of her family around the time that she suspected she had been abused. Prior to this interaction, the counselor and Janet had discussed the use of old photos in memory retrieval and Janet's possible responses to the experience (e.g. frustration if unsuccessful in memory retrieval; fear if memories did return).

> *Counselor:* Janet, pick one photo that particularly caught your eye.
> *Janet:* This one – of my whole family.
> *Counselor:* Tell me about each person in the photo.
> *Janet:* Yes, this is my mother. As you can see, she was extremely overweight. She died young – probably because she was so heavy. At the end, she could not get out of her chair. We all waited on her hand and foot. She was sort of not there, if you know what I mean. My father was always tired. He looks it there, doesn't he? He was a farmer; he worked hard all day. Came home from the field, had supper, went to bed. Probably could not deal with my mother. She was a whiner. I'm sure he thought it was stupid to take these pictures. I was 6 in this picture, my brother was 14, maybe 15. Look at the look in his eyes. Here's my older sister, Joanne.
> *Counselor:* Say more about the look in your brother's eyes.
> *Janet:* He's glaring, sullen. That's how he was. I was scared of him at times. Yet, I think I looked up to him. I remember following him around. You know, I'm sure he did things to me. I cannot remember exactly. I just know.
> *Counselor:* Where might have he hurt you?

Janet: [*points to a barn in the background of the family photo*] Here,
I think. This is where we kids would go at night to get away from
the house. I remember John was in charge of the games we played
there.

Counselor: Can you describe the inside of the barn?

Janet: It was more of an equipment shed – no animals or anything. I
remember a broken tractor, old garden tools. Stuff like that. No one
ever cleaned it out. There were mice running around. There was an
old car – a station wagon. My brother had me go in there to play the
'games.' I think he first played 'kissing' games and then 'doctor'
games. Yes, the car was the hospital. It's the doctor games that I
cannot really remember. I do remember having to kiss him, though.
He said that was what grown-ups did. I guess I would have rather
been with him than been in the house.

Janet and the counselor continued to use the album to discuss
childhood events. After each time they viewed some of the photos,
the counselor inquired as to what the experience was like for Janet.
Although working with the album was initially frightening,
memories returned slowly and periodically, at a pace that Janet did
not experience as overwhelming. However, she did occasionally
experience nightmares related to the abuse. Janet eventually
recalled more of what happened in the car – including her brother
undressing her and giving her 'exams.' These 'exams' involved him
penetrating her vagina with his fingers and other objects. In addition to memory retrieval, the photos proved helpful in provoking
discussion of her relationships with other family members,
especially her mother and father, neither of whom were available
to her at that time in her life.

Expressing, naming, and understanding feelings

Feelings often associated with the description of the abuse
experience include fear, anxiety, guilt, shame, sadness, and grief.
Just as it is important for survivors to discuss the characteristics of
the abuse experience, it is important for them to be able to express,
label, and understand these feelings.

Different types of feelings seem to play different roles in the
recovery process. Sgroi (1989a), for example, suggested that fear,
anger, and perception of loss of control are primary responses that
occur when survivors begin to acknowledge the reality of the
abuse. Survivors learn that these responses, while painful, are
tolerable. However, feelings of guilt, shame, and a sense of
damage, considered secondary responses, are subjected to what
Sgroi (1989a) refers to as contemporary denial, the denial of
current responses to the abuse experience. Although they have

acknowledged the reality of the abuse, survivors minimize its importance to block the pain of these secondary responses. Blake-White and Kline (1985) also differentiated the varied feelings experienced by survivors. They suggested that feelings of guilt and shame are often acknowledged by survivors spontaneously whereas discussion of feelings of anger and sadness, emotions 'just under the surface,' can be facilitated by the counselor. The 'stronger' emotions of terror, despair, abandonment, fear of pain, and fear of being alone continue to be denied. Counselors should validate expressed emotions, so that survivors can learn to trust and accept their feeling states, while working toward increasing the survivors' awareness of their deeper, repressed emotions.

Many survivors have experienced constricted affective lives owing to defensive processes stemming from the abuse, as well as from growing up in dysfunctional family systems where 'don't feel' was often a constant prescription. Therefore, many survivors will initially appear emotionless when describing their abuse experience (Hall and Lloyd, 1989). These individuals are often unable to identify or express their feelings when asked.

Male survivors may have especial difficulty expressing, naming, and understanding feelings. As Johanek states, 'Most men with whom we deal have learned to avoid experiencing and displaying emotions at all costs. They tend to describe events and their reactions to those events without using emotional terms' (1988: 112). Men in general are socialized to avoid expression of feelings by acting on them instead. Exploring feelings in a counseling situation may be especially threatening for male survivors.

Counseling interventions

There are several interventions that can be used to facilitate the processing of feelings, even for survivors for whom this may be especially difficult.

First, throughout the counseling process, counselors may ask clients to name and describe feelings. The following interaction exemplifies a possible counselor response when a client describes an event, but does not connect it with an affect.

> *Client:* I remember being so all alone. I was only 5, for goodness' sake. My mother and father were separating so I spent lots of time with him [an abusive babysitter]. I knew I was losing my father, and my mother in some ways too. She was so depressed.
> *Counselor:* As you describe this experience, what are you feeling?
> *Client:* Sad, incredibly sad. I was only 5. I was losing everyone.

Second, when survivors do respond with feeling statements,

counselors can acknowledge the client's feelings with empathic responses:

> *Client:* The devastation I felt when my mother found out was tremendous. Even now, years later when I see her I want to fall through the floor; I just want to be invisible. I was her perfect angel and I was sleeping with her husband. I would have rather died than let her know what a slut I was.
>
> *Counselor:* As a child you experienced great shame and it is a feeling that's stayed with you all these years, still causing you pain.

Third, for clients who are unable to name or express feelings, counselors may suggest that others in the survivor's situation may feel certain emotions, such as anger, fear, or sadness, and inquire if the survivor might not be experiencing any of these feelings. The counselor should mention several feelings so that the survivors do not experience the counselor telling them 'how to feel.' The following interaction includes a counselor response to a client who was having difficulty naming her feelings:

> *Client:* He would feel me every chance he got. When I walked by him in the hall he would corner me and feel my breasts or my legs. I was never safe. He was a perverted creep.
>
> *Counselor:* How did you feel when he did this?
>
> *Client:* I'm not sure.
>
> *Counselor:* Some teenagers in that situation might have felt angry or frustrated or trapped, or even frightened. Did you feel any of those things?
>
> *Client:* I was not allowed to feel anything. I was probably mad, deep down inside, but I would never say so. Then, I would have gotten beaten.

Fourth, when working with clients whose families, or society, discourage the expression of feelings, counselors may explore this issue with survivors prior to addressing affect in counseling. The following interaction is with a male survivor:

> *Client:* He was my own brother. I looked up to him. When I realized what he did . . . [*starts to cry*] See, I'm still a wimp today.
>
> *Counselor:* It sounds like you've gotten the message that 'real men don't cry.' That message prevents you from allowing yourself to feel sad about a sad thing that happened to you. Where did that message come from?

Client responses to the focus on sexual abuse

Although the focus on the sexual abuse experience early in counseling can provide an explanation for survivors' distress and therefore hope for recovery, the processes described in this chapter can also lead to painful emotional responses as the minimization lifts and survivors become aware of the impact of the abuse experience on their lives. Counselors must be prepared to deal with client experiences of intense emotional responses, self-destructive behaviors, and post-traumatic symptomatology. Generally, this includes assessing clients' safety, helping them understand the role these responses play in recovery, and allowing clients control over the pace of their treatment.

Intense emotional responses
When clients first begin to focus on their sexual abuse, they may experience intense feelings, such as anxiety, fear, depression, or shame, which they perceive as overwhelming. One survivor in the incest healing study (Draucker, 1992) discussed her response when she first began to connect her current experiences with her childhood abuse:

> It was really scary in one sense because my feelings became real and I wasn't – I couldn't sleep – I was dealing with a lot of nightmares. I couldn't stay by myself and it was like the worst thing, of going into therapy or counseling. Everything just became so .real. And it became such a controlling force in my life at that time.

A useful heuristic related to the regulation of intense emotional responses is Cole and Barney's (1987) concept of the therapeutic window. These authors discussed the two major phases of the stress response cycle. The denial phase is characterized by symptoms such as amnesia or repression, minimization, and other forms of withdrawal. The intrusive phase is characterized by intense affect, perceptual experiences (i.e. hallucinations, nightmares) and autonomic physical responses (e.g. tremors, sweating). Between these phases is the therapeutic window, characterized by moderate distress and manageable symptomatology. If survivors' emotional states are within their therapeutic windows, exploration of abuse issues is effective. However, if survivors experience too much stress from dealing with abuse material, they will move into one of the phases of the stress response cycle. When in the denial phase, their defenses prohibit processing the abuse material, whereas when in the intrusive phase their daily functioning is disrupted. The counselor's task is to 'judge carefully the amount and exposure to . . . memories and affects the survivors can tolerate. That is, the therapist should monitor the "dosage" of intensity and duration so that it is of therapeutically manageable proportions' (Cole and Barney, 1987: 603).

Counseling interventions

Several counseling interventions can be used to facilitate the management of the intense emotional reactions that survivors may have to the focus on the sexual abuse experience.

First, it is important for the counselor to discuss these possible reactions with the client at the beginning of counseling. If clients are informed that such intense reactions can be expected when the sexual abuse becomes a focus, that counseling almost always involves 'getting worse before getting better,' and that their current emotional responses will not last for ever, clients experience less hopelessness and feel less overwhelmed.

Second, it is also helpful for the client to know that an intense emotional response to their current experiences does not mean that they are 'going crazy,' but that they have just embarked on a painful and frightening process.

Third, and perhaps most importantly, the counselor needs to be available to the client during this time, as the most effective way for survivors to deal with these feelings is to express them and to receive support, validation, and reassurance. If there are significant others (e.g. spouses) who are supportive and invested in the survivor's treatment, these individuals can also be involved in assisting the survivor during this time.

To begin these three interventions, counselors may offer survivors the following statement shortly after implementing the sexual abuse contract:

> Often, when survivors focus on their sexual abuse experience, they may begin to experience very intense emotions. Sometimes they begin to believe they are getting worse, or that they will have these feelings for ever. They may even worry that the intensity of the feelings means that they are 'going insane.' Actually, the feelings are part of the process of healing. They are temporary and indicate that the survivor is doing therapeutic work. I will be available to help you deal with these feelings if they arise.

Fourth, counselors may discuss the concept of the therapeutic window (Cole and Barney, 1987) with survivors in terms they can understand. Counselors might say, for example:

> Although painful feelings are necessary for healing, we can discuss the abuse material at a pace that does not feel overwhelming for you. If you feel our discussions are too stressful or emotional to be helpful, we'll slow down, and if you start to feel stuck or don't feel anything, we'll begin to explore the abuse in more depth. It's this middle ground where the most productive work gets done.

Once clients grasp this concept, counselors can 'check in' with survivors at the beginning and end of each session to find out where the survivors believe they are in their 'therapeutic windows.'

Trauma symptomatology
Many survivors, after discussing their experience of childhood sexual abuse, will experience trauma symptoms (e.g. flashbacks, nightmares, perceptual disturbances) as focusing on the abuse experience precipitates the return of repressed memories and, as trauma theory suggests, the re-enactment of the trauma. The experience of trauma symptomatology is actually a necessary and therapeutic part of the healing process, representing the loosening of defenses. As Sgroi has pointed out, the treatment goal related to these symptoms is 'not to suppress flashbacks or disturbing memories but rather to experience them and process them as a necessary step in coming to terms with and moving beyond the entire victimization experience' (1989a: 116).

Counseling interventions to address trauma symptomatology are quite similar to those used to address intense emotional responses. Counselors can discuss these symptoms with survivors, acknowledge how frightening they can be, stress their temporary nature, and teach survivors how to control them.

Grounding techniques – methods used to keep in touch with reality – can be used to manage trauma symptoms (Blake-White and Kline, 1985; Cole and Barney, 1987). These techniques include physical methods, such as planting one's feet firmly on the ground or grasping the arms of one's chair during a flashback, or cognitive techniques, such as repeating one's name, age, and current location to remind oneself that one is not actually in the childhood situation.

Survivors can also begin to learn to control the course of their nightmares. For example, if survivors have nightmares of being chased by an intruder, they can be instructed to tell themselves, before drifting off to sleep at night, that instead of running away in their dream, they will stop and turn and order the intruder to leave and he and she will do so. They therefore begin to affect the outcome of their nightmares.

Self-destructive behaviors
Intense affective reactions to the focus on the sexual abuse may be accompanied by self-destructive behaviors (e.g. suicide attempts, self-mutilation, bingeing), especially by clients who have a history of such behaviors. This possibly can be dealt with directly by the counselor by assisting clients to provide for their safety. The following counselor response may be helpful for clients whom the

counselor has assessed as being at risk of self-harm:

> The process we've agreed to undertake [the focus on sexual abuse] can be long and painful and you've shared with me that at times when you experience pain you do things to hurt yourself. Therefore, we need to find ways you can keep yourself safe before we start.

Survivors and counselors can determine and agree upon a plan of action specifying what the client will do if he or she becomes at risk of engaging in self-destructive behaviors. For example, no-suicide contracts with specific plans in the event of suicidal ideation can be helpful. These plans can include self-control techniques (e.g. becoming involved in some activity), calling the counselor or a hotline, or going to the emergency room of a hospital in the event of imminent danger. Designing such explicit agreements between counselor and client shows the counselor's concern for the client's safety while giving the client responsibility for his or her actions by providing specific guidelines for managing self-destructive urges.

Aggression against others
Although the issue of survivors and abuse of others as a long-term effect will be discussed later, increased aggression as a response to the focus on the abuse will be mentioned here. This may be a special concern for male survivors. Bruckner and Johnson (1987), who described conducting group therapy with male survivors, noted that the group members expressed intense anger following disclosure. This anger was often accompanied by plans for retribution, including physical assault on offenders.

Counseling survivors who react to disclosure with aggressive impulses initially involves an assessment of their potential to harm others. This must be done concurrently with validation of their angry feelings. A helpful counselor response to a survivor who threatens or implies intent to harm another might be:

> I appreciate the rage you feel toward your offender. You have every right to feel anger that intensely. However, I am concerned you are considering harming him, which will also cause you trouble eventually. Let's discuss your plans.

A longer-term counseling goal for the survivor with aggressive impulses involves anger management. Clients are taught to express anger verbally and constructively. Assertiveness training is a useful counseling technique for this purpose.

Substance abuse
Many survivors present with problems of substance abuse, which may be exacerbated during disclosure and the early phases of

counseling. For survivors who are actively abusing substances, treatment for sexual abuse must be preceded by a period of sobriety (Skorina and Kovach, 1986). Counseling for abuse issues is usually most effective if it follows involvement in a chemical-dependency treatment program, such as Alcoholics Anonymous (AA). This stipulation may be part of the sexual abuse contract so that the counselor can acknowledge and validate the importance of the sexual abuse while emphasizing that sobriety is a necessary prerequisite for recovery.

Sexual abuse survivors are often particularly resistant to involvement in self-help groups such as Alcoholics Anonymous, and several counseling interventions are recommended to deal with this resistance (Skorina and Kovach, 1986). The first step of an AA program is the 'admission of powerlessness over alcohol and life' (ibid.: 23), a terrifying prospect for survivors of sexual abuse. Counselors can address this issue with survivors by discussing the difference between being powerless over a substance and being powerless over one's body or psyche, stressing that admission of powerlessness over a substance is actually a way of gaining control. Because another block to survivors' participation in an AA program is lack of trust, counselors can assist them to find 'home groups' and sponsors (i.e. peers from AA with a history of sobriety who provide personal support) who are sensitive to abuse issues. If the survivor is a woman, the choice of a mixed-gender or all-female group and a female sponsor would probably be the most appropriate. Further, the invitation to 'tell one's story' in an AA meeting may be experienced as intrusive by the survivor, so it is helpful for the counselor to assist the survivor to prepare for this in advance.

Providing for general self-care

Even survivors who are not self-destructive in one of the ways discussed above may have a tendency to neglect their self-care needs (e.g. they may have poor eating habits or a lack of pleasurable activities) during this early phase of counseling. This may be due to feelings of lack of self-worth, which can be exacerbated following disclosure. One of the participants in the incest healing study (Draucker, 1992), for example, described how healing for her involved learning to attend to her personal needs:

> I also learned to do little things that make me feel better about myself, like – really small things but before I go to bed at night maybe I'll fall into bed and I'll think – 'Well, wait, you forgot to brush your teeth and wash your face. Get up and do it!' Whereas before I'd lay in bed and say 'Well, so what?' You'll get a cavity; so maybe your face will break out.

Counselors can address this issue early in treatment with the following response:

> You are starting on a process which could be very painful and there will be need for you to be able to take care of yourself. What are the ways you would like to do this?

Constructing a self-care plan may be something as simple as an agreement to treat oneself to a desired article of clothing, or to take a warm bubble bath after a particularly difficult session, or as comprehensive as a nutrition and exercise plan to accompany the counseling process. Although providing for self-care typically becomes easier when survivors are further along in the healing process, making a commitment to a reasonable plan early in treatment suggests to clients that they can take action to tolerate the painful aspects of the counseling process.

Case example

The following case exemplifies the process of focusing on the abuse experience in counseling following disclosure of childhood sexual abuse. Susan, a 40-year-old woman, sought counseling because she was distressed regarding the 'direction' her current relationship with her significant other, Ray, aged 52, had taken. Susan had dated Ray steadily for four years and had hoped to marry him. She reported their sex life was 'OK,' although she stated she had always been inorgasmic. Ray was not interested in a 'commitment' such as marriage, claiming his prior marriage had been 'hell' and he was still supporting his two teenage sons. Susan stated that she had accepted this but was very upset to learn recently that Ray had been dating another woman.

Susan had worked for twenty-one years as a secretary and a bookkeeper for a small local industry. She indicated that she did very well at her job, but sometimes felt 'pushed around' by her boss. Describing herself as a 'shrinking violet,' she reported that she did not have any close friends. She had little contact with her elderly parents who lived approximately one and a half hours' drive away. Susan stated that she had never been married but had been in two long-term relationships prior to meeting Ray. She claimed both men were 'losers,' both were alcoholic, and one had been physically abusive to her. She reported being very grateful that Ray was 'different' from these men. Susan denied using any alcohol or drugs, but she did discuss a significant weight problem and admitted to occasional bingeing. She had sought counseling on several prior occasions and reported feeling somewhat better about herself after each attempt at counseling.

When asked about childhood sexual abuse during the initial interview, Susan readily revealed that she had been molested by an uncle on several occasions over three summers from the ages 9 to 11. Her uncle had a farm that she and her younger brother visited during school vacations. She stated he 'taught' her to perform oral intercourse on him and told her she would need to know how to do this to boys when she got older. She reported being 'disgusted' by the experience but preferred the freedom she experienced on the farm to the strict rules (e.g. early bedtime, many 'chores,' frequent church attendance) of her parents, whom she described as 'strict fundamentalists.' Susan described her parents, who were neither physically nor sexually abusive, as 'good people' who worked hard but who did not show any emotion.

After one summer when the abuse was particularly bad, she and her brother never returned to the farm nor did they have much further contact with this uncle. Susan always wondered if this was because her mother 'found out' what had happened and recalled being very worried that this was the case. However, nothing was ever said about the visits to the farm. Susan stated that she had put the abuse behind her and had forgiven her uncle because he was 'sick.'

Susan is an example of a survivor who had not repressed memories of the abuse and who readily disclosed the abuse on inquiry, but who minimized the impact both the abuse and the family dynamics surrounding the abuse had had on her life. The following interaction between Susan and her counselor illustrates the process of minimization:

> *Counselor:* When an older person, such as your uncle, uses a little girl to meet his own needs, this can be a hurtful experience.
>
> *Susan:* Well, yes it did hurt me. I felt like the tramp, though. Mostly I hoped my mother would not find out. It was so long ago though. He was probably sick. I do not think he meant to hurt me. I'm sure I'm over it. In fact, to be perfectly truthful, I really don't like to talk about it.
>
> *Counselor:* Yes, these experiences can be hard to discuss. Initially, talking about them can feel like 'digging up the past' for no reason. And yet because these experiences can be hurtful, they are important to address. Often, an experience like the one you describe could be affecting you in ways you might not be aware of. To avoid talking about it, therefore, can interfere with really understanding what's going on with you today.
>
> *Susan:* How would that be true for me?
>
> *Counselor:* I'm not really sure right now. We can explore that question together. Let me give you a *general* example, though. An experience of sexual abuse can destroy a child's trust in the adults in her life

because she is supposed to be able to depend on those adults to protect her safety. Having learned not to trust others as a child, she cannot trust others as an adult. She therefore stays away from other people and may experience a good deal of loneliness. Your abuse may have affected you in very different ways, but that's one example of how such a childhood experience can affect one's later life.

Susan: Well, my experience with my uncle could I suppose have something to do with my sexual problem, and maybe even with my track record with men.

Susan agreed to explore her sexual abuse experience, stating she had 'nothing to lose.' However, she then left counseling at Ray's request. He told Susan she 'need not dig up the past.' Four months later Susan returned to counseling, informing the counselor that Ray had left her for another woman and that she had started to think more and more about her relationship with her uncle and her 'poor choice of men.'

At this point, she and her counselor contracted to focus on her childhood experiences and to explore the connections between these experiences and her current problems. This process did involve a review of the sexual abuse experience, which was introduced by the counselor in the following manner:

Counselor: Susan, I know you shared with me that it is very hard for you to talk about what actually happened with your uncle. However, describing that experience is an important part of the healing process. It helps me to appreciate and understand what you went through as a little girl and helps you begin to sort through what happened and begin to make sense of it. We can go at your pace and stop whenever you feel the need to. Are you feeling ready to start telling me what happened?

Susan: Yes, I am ready. I just do not really know where to begin.

Counselor: Why don't you start with the first incident you remember.

Susan: I think I was 9 – maybe 10. I had been at the farm only a day. I was really happy to be there. Uncle Bob treated me real nice. He had bought me some new dresses. Anyway, I was in the barn. He came out and told me how pretty I was. No one ever said that to me. Come to think of it no one does now either. [*Laughs*] Even though I was skinny then I was pretty homely. Anyway, he told me he was going to teach me how to kiss as boys would soon be asking me to kiss them – because I was pretty.

Included in the description of the abuse experience, which continued intermittently for many sessions, were discussions of other abuse incidents, which involved progressively more invasive sexual activities; techniques used by her uncle to continue to engage Susan in the abuse; her memories of her childhood reactions to the abuse; her relationship with her parents at the time of the abuse; and the circumstances in which the abuse stopped.

Although Susan had initially dissociated much affect from the abuse experience, she began to respond readily when the counselor asked her to name and describe her feelings. She remembered feeling like a dirty girl and she reported feeling guilty because, although she hated the sexual activity, she did enjoy the attention from her uncle. Mostly, she reported fearing her parents would discover what had happened. She imagined they would completely reject her or bring her 'sins' to the attention of their minister. Therefore, she felt a good deal of shame that she had carried with her into adulthood. Betrayal, by both her parents and her trusted uncle, emerged as a key issue for her.

Susan denied experiencing any post-traumatic stress symptoms as she began to discuss the details of the abuse by her uncle. She did report a dramatic increase in her food consumption, although she denied bingeing. She and her counselor worked on a self-care contract, which included her participation in a Weight Watchers' group; a short, daily walk; and a 'no binge' agreement.

After one particularly difficult session, however, during which Susan described her rage at her mother because Susan had not felt able to talk to her about the abuse, Susan reported a serious bingeing episode. Although the counselor reiterated her concerns related to self-care, she and Susan interpreted this incident as Susan's attempt to see if she could violate a rule (her no-bingeing agreement) and tell her counselor without being rejected. This was something she could not do with her mother when she was a child. No further bingeing occurred and although Susan's weight fluctuated, she did consistently attend her weight program and follow her program of moderate exercise.

After this incident, Susan did begin to connect her present experiences with her current distress. She recognized that as a child she could not express her needs for either attention or for protection in her family because she considered herself to be 'bad' and was therefore not worthy of having either of these needs met. She began to see her choice of men as being related to her belief that she did not deserve better, and her sexual dysfunction related to her belief that she did not deserve sexual pleasure.

For Susan, the focus on sexual abuse in counseling involved first coming to believe that the abuse was significant and that it had had an impact on her life. She contracted with her counselor to explore her sexual abuse experience and was able to describe it detail. She could begin to express her feelings related to the abuse. The self-destructive behavior that accompanied this affective response was addressed with a self-care contract and an interpretation of the behavior as it related to her sexual experience.

4

Reinterpreting the Sexual Abuse Experience from an Adult Perspective

Once survivors have retrieved and validated memories of the abuse and fully described their experience, counselors may assist them in reinterpreting the abuse experience from an adult perspective. This process is important because memories of the abuse are often repressed at a time when the child's cognitive skills are still developing, so survivors retain a 'child's concept of the event' (Blake-White and Kline, 1985: 398). Survivors especially tend to interpret their role in the abuse from their childhood perspective, believing they were to blame for the abuse because they were 'bad' or 'dirty.' These interpretations, which often have not been verbally shared with others and therefore remain unchallenged, and which at times may have been reinforced by messages from others, contribute to the shame and guilt experienced by survivors. Survivors often judge their behavior in the abuse situation by attributing to themselves, as children, the adult resources of freedom of choice, social support, and the power of reasoning. This results in the belief that they could have controlled the abuse. Counselors may assist survivors to use their adult cognitive skills to reinterpret their childhood experiences based on an understanding of their stage of development and the dynamics of their family at the time of the abuse. The issues that are important for survivors to reframe in this way and counseling procedures that can facilitate this process are discussed in this chapter.

Issues to reframe from adult perspective

Attribution of blame

Most authors who have addressed the counseling needs of adult survivors of childhood sexual abuse have indicated that survivors' self-blame for the abuse is a key therapeutic issue (Briere, 1989; Faria and Belohlavek, 1984; Gelinas, 1983; Hall and Lloyd, 1989; Westerlund, 1983). Survivors generally believe that they were responsible for the abuse. Herman has proposed that this belief reflects the attitudes of society that blame the daughter, or at times the mother, for sexual abuse that occurs in the family. She describes this myth: 'Ensnared by the charms of a small temptress, or driven to her arms by a frigid, unloving wife, Poor Father can hardly help himself, or so his defenders would have us believe' (1981: 36). Herman argues that the concept of the 'Seductive Daughter' is culturally embedded in religious traditions (e.g. the biblical story of Lot and his daughters), in popular literature (e.g. the story of 'Lolita'), and even in some clinical literature.

General societal prescriptions also reinforce self-blame in survivors. Westerlund (1983) listed three attitudes of society that contribute to the self-blame of the female survivor: females 'incite' male sexual behaviors; 'boys will be boys'; and it is the responsibility of females to control male sexuality. One participant in the incest healing study (Draucker, 1992) stated:

> Your parents teach you that you are responsible if you get pregnant or if you have sex with a boy. You are the one that's responsible, you're the one that's in control of the situation and, you know, if your dad's taking advantage of you, you are responsible.

Often, survivors as children had received direct messages from the offender that they were to blame for the abuse (e.g. the abuse was a punishment for being 'bad'). Survivors might also have received blaming messages from significant others. Many survivors relate experiences of being punished for their 'naughty' behavior when they disclosed the abuse. Undoubtedly, incestuous family dynamics, as outlined by Gelinas (1983), would also reinforce their self-blame. Due to the process of parentification, incest survivors learned to assume responsibility for the feelings, needs, and behaviors of others. Male survivors often blame themselves, not necessarily for instigating the abuse, but for failing to protect themselves against the offender (Struve, 1990). This often results in internalized anger or compensatory behaviors to regain control (e.g. aggression, exaggerated masculine behaviors). These beliefs are rooted in societal prescriptions that males are not victims and should be powerful enough to protect themselves from the intrusion and aggression of others.

Reframing the attribution of blame from an adult perspective involves survivors coming to accept that the offender, not themselves, was responsible for the abusive sexual activity. This is true regardless of the 'engagement strategies' (e.g. threat, bribery, force, 'brainwashing') employed by the offender (Sgroi and Bunk, 1988). Children, by virtue of their stage of psychosocial and cognitive development and their dependent position within the family structure, are unable to make a free choice regarding involvement in sexual activity. It is the responsibility of the adult, or the more powerful other, to resist engaging in exploitative sexual activities with the child, regardless of the child's behavior.

Childhood sexual responsiveness
Many survivors responded physically with pleasure or arousal during the abuse experience, and therefore concluded that as children they had enjoyed and sought the experience. Males, who are often the victims of same-sex abuse, may believe that such responses represent latent homosexual desires (Struve, 1990). Reframing the issue of sexual responsiveness from an adult perspective involves survivors realizing that the sensations they experienced as children were natural physiological reactions to sexual stimulation. Such responses differ from sexual arousal in adulthood, when mature emotional and cognitive factors are able to influence one's enjoyment of a sexual experience. Arousal in childhood does not indicate that the child either sought or enjoyed the sexual experience.

Issues of attention and affection
Similarly, many survivors enjoyed the attention or affection associated with their abuse and concluded that as children they had sought or desired the sexual activity. Often, given the dysfunctional nature of their family systems, the attention or affection they received from the offender may well have been the only emotional nurturance they received. In fact, special attention is often effective as an 'engagement strategy' (Sgroi and Bunk, 1988) because the child's life is so often void of caring from others. Reframing the issue of the seeking of attention and affection from an adult perspective involves survivors coming to believe that the need for attention and affection from a significant adult is basic to all children and that children will naturally try to meet this need in any ways that are open to them. It was emotional nurturance from an adult that the survivors sought as children, not the accompanying sexual activity.

Why me?
Survivors often reach adulthood with the belief that they were singled out for the abuse because of inherent characteristics they possessed as children. This belief is especially prevalent if they were the only victim within their family. Some survivors assume they were basically bad or 'naughty' and some assume they were especially 'sexy,' although often in an 'evil' (Herman, 1981) or

dirty way. Reframing the 'why me?' issue from an adult perspective involves survivors coming to appreciate that they were chosen as a victim, not because of any inherent personality characteristics, but because of factors related to the offender's motives or to the family dynamics (e.g. as the oldest child, a female victim was the most likely to be parentified; the child was at an age that met the offender's emotional needs; the child was the most 'available'). To dispute the belief that as children they were inherently sexually provocative, adult survivors must appreciate their 'level of sexual knowledge and awareness before the start of the abuse' (Hall and Lloyd, 1989: 112), thereby realizing that initially they did not have the capacity for sexual seductiveness. Seductive behaviors are not the cause of the abuse; rather, these behaviors are typically learned as a result of a sexually abusive experience.

Having kept the secret

Many survivors experience self-blame, not because they believe they instigated the abuse or enjoyed the experience, but because they never told anyone of the abuse and therefore did not 'stop' it. This concern is especially salient if the abuse went on for a long time, if the child was older when the abuse started, if the 'engagement strategies' (Sgroi and Bunk, 1988) did not involve the use of force, and if the child had no role in stopping the abuse. Reframing 'secret keeping' from an adult perspective involves survivors considering their assumptions as children regarding the consequences of disclosure (e.g. punishment, family break-up, disbelief by significant others, rejection by the offender). It is also important for survivors to consider that telling others, a proactive behavior, was often simply not in their behavioral repertoire as a child. Also, disclosure would have required the availability of receptive significant others, something many survivors were not privileged to have. As one survivor in the incest healing study (Draucker, 1992) stated:

> even at the time it never occurred to me to tell anybody. I didn't know who to tell, I didn't know how to tell, I didn't know what the consequences of telling would have been, I just wanted it to stop. But it never occurred to me to tell. That given the way I was raised in the household, no, I wouldn't have told. I just wouldn't have. Again, that's me being a normal little kid if you will.

Counseling procedures for reframing

There are several counseling procedures that can be used to facilitate the reinterpretation of the sexual abuse experience from an adult perspective. These include techniques to challenge currently held beliefs, techniques used to reinforce survivors' perceptions of themselves as children at the time of the abuse, the reinforcement of new beliefs through exposure to other survivors, and the reinforcement of new beliefs by vicarious and actual interactions with the offender or the family of origin.

Challenging beliefs

A basic technique for addressing a belief held by a survivor that leads to shame and guilt is a cognitive challenge (Sgroi and Bunk, 1988), which is a response made by a counselor that disputes the survivor's belief and, using adult reasoning, describes the reality of the abuse. Cognitive challenges are exemplified in the following counselor interventions. The first intervention challenges a belief that a survivor caused the abuse because she was flirtatious and the second challenges a belief that a survivor enjoyed the abuse because he was sexually stimulated.

> *Harriet:* I think I was a flirt even when I was that young. If I had said something he would have stopped. I do think I must have been at least partly to blame. Why else would I feel like such a slut?
>
> *Counselor:* A 5-year-old child cannot really flirt as we think of flirting because at that age she does not understand adult sexual behaviors enough to know how to flirt. Also, as a 5-year-old child you could not be responsible for what happened. You were totally dependent on your father and were unable to say no to his requests. As an adult, it was his responsibility to protect you, not to exploit you to meet his needs.

***

> *Jonathon:* When I talked to him [the offender] about it [the abuse], he had a good point. In some ways, it felt good to me, the sex I mean. I mean I knew it was wrong and I was scared, but it felt good. I don't know how to say this – but at times I ended up, you know, responding when he touched my private parts. He's right, I must have liked it somewhat.
>
> *Counselor:* The response you felt when your brother touched your genitals was a normal, physiological response to stimulation, not an indication that you sought or desired the sexual activity.

Questioning techniques can also be used to challenge survivors' beliefs related to their responsibility for the abuse (Hall and Lloyd, 1989). For example, to challenge the belief that survivors wanted the abuse because they did nothing to stop it, counselors may ask them what they might have done to stop the abuse, what might have happened if they took this action, whom they would have told, and how this person is most likely to have responded. Such a line of questioning allows survivors to begin to reason themselves that, as children, they did not have the resources, either cognitively or emotionally, to stop the abuse; that to attempt to do so would have resulted in feared consequences; and that they might not have had supportive individuals in their lives who would have been receptive to disclosure.

The following client–counselor interaction involves a line of questioning to address a survivor's belief that she was responsible for the abuse because she never told anyone that it was occurring.

> *Mary:* The abuse went on for almost four years. I was 8 when it first started – but about 12 when it stopped. I was almost a teenager for heaven's sake. I could have done something, you'd think, to stop it, if I had really wanted to.
>
> *Counselor:* What might have you done to stop it?
>
> *Mary:* Tell him. Stop it or I'll tell the rest of the world.
>
> *Counselor:* What might he have done if you had done that?
>
> *Mary:* Deny it. Everyone would have believed him. Famous attorney that he was. What a joke! Do you know he was president of the Lions Club [a local civics organization]?
>
> *Counselor:* As a child then you realized telling him to stop or you would tell others would not have been successful in stopping the abuse?
>
> *Mary:* Also remember he had a violent temper. I was afraid of him. He would beat us for forgetting to bring in the garbage. What would he do if I blew the whistle?
>
> *Counselor:* So you believed, if you told, not only would no one believe you, but you would probably have gotten beaten. What else do you think you could have done to stop it?
>
> *Mary:* Telling my mother would have been a joke. She couldn't stop him from beating her. She certainly couldn't stop him from coming on to me. I suppose if I really wanted out I could have run away.
>
> *Counselor:* Where would have you gone?
>
> *Mary:* Probably to the streets. I'd be a hooker now. Lots of us turn out that way, you know.
>
> *Counselor:* So even though the abuse went on for four years, until you were 12, as a kid you had no real options for stopping what was happening to you. If you told, no one would have believed you or you would have gotten beaten. Your mother was no help and you really had no place to go if you did run away. That's a hard situation for a 12 year-old, isn't it?
>
> *Mary:* Ya, I guess it is.

Cognitive restructuring

Jehu et al. (1986) recommended cognitive restructuring as an approach to address beliefs that survivors hold that contribute to their current feelings of guilt. The counselor begins by explaining the process of cognitive restructuring, which is based on the principle that beliefs influence feelings and that if beliefs are distorted, then the resultant feelings can be distressing, leading to behavioral or emotional problems. Jehu et al. recommended giving the survivor an 'everyday' example of how beliefs lead to feelings that lead to behavioral responses. The counselor might give this example:

> If Joe concludes that he was turned down for a job because of basic incompetence, he will feel depressed, and it is unlikely that he will apply for another similar job. If, on the other hand, Joe believes he was turned down due to unusually stiff competition, he will feel mildly discouraged, but is likely to keep trying for other similar positions.

The next stage in cognitive restructuring is assisting clients to identify their beliefs, which are often automatic or unconscious, when they experience distress. Techniques to facilitate this process include reviewing the sequence of events leading to the distressing affect, re-enacting a distressing event in a role play, using relaxation and imagery to re-experience the event, responding to questionnaires that outline distorted beliefs commonly experienced by survivors, and keeping a journal to record one's thoughts.

In the following interaction, the survivor, a 20-year-old college student, Jane, and the counselor work on identifying Jane's beliefs that result in depressed feelings whenever she visits her mother. Jane had disclosed her experience of childhood sexual abuse by her stepfather to her mother one year prior to this interaction.

> *Jane:* Every time I go home I end up feeling awful. This time I cried for two days when I got back. I can't understand why. My mom has been great. She's supported me all the way. If I want to talk about it [the abuse] she will. If I don't she won't mention it. I know from group that most other mothers are not that great. Why do I feel so sad when we are together?
>
> *Counselor:* When, during this visit, did you notice yourself feeling sad?
>
> *Jane:* I made note of when this time. It was Saturday night. I had a date with a high school boyfriend. When we said goodbye to my mom she looked sad, lonely. I guess I started to feel bad then. Guilty somehow.
>
> *Counselor:* What were you thinking at that point?
>
> *Jane:* That I'm getting better, getting on with my life. She's all alone.
>
> *Counselor:* What thoughts did you have about her being alone?
>
> *Jane:* That if I had not brought this all up, she would not be alone now.
>
> *Counselor:* The sadness results from your belief that your mom, whom you care about, is lonely. The guilt, and probably the depression you feel when you go home, results from the belief that you were responsible for that.
>
> *Jane:* Yes, I guess I do believe that.

Assisting survivors to recognize distortions in their beliefs is the next step in the cognitive restructuring process. Survivors are taught commonly exhibited thought distortions (e.g. all-or-nothing thinking, overgeneralization, mislabeling, emotional reasoning) and are assisted in identifying these distortions in their own thought processes. The authors (Jehu et al., 1986) gave as an example the negative belief that one was responsible for sexual abuse in childhood because it lasted a long time and was perpetrated without the use of force. They suggested that this belief is due to the common cognitive distortions of personalization (assuming responsibility for events for which one is not to blame) and arbitrary inference (drawing negative conclusions not supported by facts).

The next stage, exploring alternatives, involves assisting the client in replacing distorted beliefs with more accurate, realistic beliefs. This procedure can involve providing factual information (e.g. statistics on the prevalence of childhood sexual abuse, discussion of the dynamics of the incestuous family), encouraging analysis of the evidence that supports or disproves the survivors' conclusions, shifting from the subjective to the objective perspective (e.g. asking the survivor to judge 'other survivors' in their position), and assisting clients with the process of reattribution of responsibility for the abuse. Alternative beliefs to the belief that one was responsible for the abuse because it lasted a long time would include beliefs that the survivor was indoctrinated to believe that she was supposed to please adults; that as a child she badly needed the offender's attention; and that if she told others of the abuse, she might be disbelieved, ignored, or punished.

Jane and her counselor focused on recognizing the distortion in her belief that she caused her mother to be lonely and on exploring alternative beliefs by 'analyzing evidence.' Jane had read a list of the common distortions and decided that her belief distortions included personalization and arbitrary inference. The following interaction involved a discussion of the arbitrary inference distortion.

> *Jane:* I assumed my mother left my stepfather because of what I told her. When I read about 'arbitrary inference,' I thought that might be applicable because I really do not know why she left him. We have never talked about that.
>
> *Counselor:* What evidence do you have that your disclosure was the reason for their separation?
>
> *Jane:* Timing. It happened shortly, well about six months, after I told her. Why else?
>
> *Counselor:* Let's discuss the 'why else?' Are there other reasons they may have separated?
>
> *Jane:* Well, they really never got along. He was always away on business. She always stuck with him though. She thought to leave him would make her a two-time loser. She never got over that my dad left her.

Counselor: So leaving him was something she considered before your disclosure . . . .
Jane: Yes, but she never did it. So I still have to think . . . .
Counselor: What might be some other *possible* reasons she left him, now?
Jane: There must be others, I know. I just assumed it was me. You know, maybe I can ask her.

Jane did ask her mother why she had left her husband. Her mother revealed that Jane's decision had precipitated her action, but reassured Jane that it did not cause it. The stepfather had been having a relationship with another woman, about which Jane's mother had known for several years. The 'other woman' had a 5-year-old daughter. Jane's mother left her husband and then told this woman of her husband's abuse of Jane in order to protect the little girl. Jane's mother had done this with the support of her own therapist, with whom she had been working since Jane's disclosure. She did not tell Jane about the other woman because her mother believed Jane had 'been through enough.' Jane's mother was lonely, but felt she had taken 'healthy steps.'

For Jane, cognitive restructuring involved identifying the belief which led to her depressed feelings whenever she went home from college, determining the distortion in the belief, and challenging the belief both by considering other possible alternatives with her counselor and by actually 'analyzing the evidence' by talking with her mother. Jane was thus able to see that the separation was not caused by her disclosure *per se* and that what she considered a negative event in her mother's life was actually a positive, although painful, event for her mother.

Dealing with guilt

Sgroi and Bunk (1988) have pointed out that survivors' feelings of guilt are often resistant to cognitive challenges. They have reported that while survivors may feel less ashamed about their role in the abuse situation in response to these challenges, they continue to experience significant guilt. For these survivors, guilt may serve a protective function that prevents them from being overwhelmed by feelings of powerlessness. The assumption that the abuse occurred because they wanted it in some way may be less aversive initially than accepting that the abuse was completely out of their control. Therefore, being told by counselors that survivors are not to blame and 'should not feel guilty' can result in overwhelming anxiety. It would be more therapeutic to *acknowledge* their guilt and to suggest that the guilt generally begins to subside when survivors begin to feel better. This reinforces the idea that the survivors' feelings are under their control and can be abandoned only when they no longer need them (Sgroi and Bunk, 1988).

Sgroi and Bunk (1988) discussed the use of a therapeutic technique that they have found to be helpful in addressing the guilt experienced by survivors. They ask survivors to list everything they have done since the beginning of their abuse about which they feel guilty. The survivors and the counselor (or group therapy members) 'negotiate' which of those items constitute legitimate guilt (i.e. what most people would feel guilty about) and which constitute inappropriate guilt (i.e. what most people would not feel guilty about). Hurting a sibling at the time of the abuse would result in legitimate guilt, whereas accepting responsibility for the break-up of the family following disclosure would result in inappropriate guilt. This activity helps survivors to identify the specific aspects of their guilt (rather than experiencing it as a pervasive, consuming affect), and allows them to receive feedback from others regarding the causes of their guilt. Often, survivors plan 'expiatory' actions (e.g. asking for forgiveness, apologizing) for behaviors that have resulted in legitimate guilt. Survivors are thereby empowered to experience less guilt related to behaviors leading to legitimate guilt and a gradual lessening of inappropriate guilt related to the sexual abuse experience.

Respecting survivors' loyalty to their families
Gelinas (1983) has discussed another issue to consider in facilitating the reattribution of blame, and that is the need for the counselor to respect survivors' loyalty to their family of origin, including the offender. Survivors may continue to feel protective, and in some cases loving, to those who were responsible for their abuse or to other family members who were present when the abuse occurred. If family loyalties are ignored by counselors and they prematurely encourage the expression of anger, survivors' resistance to the re-attribution process will increase. It is important that survivors have the opportunity to express their positive feelings toward the offender and the family. If these feelings are accepted by the counselor, survivors can then explore the offender's responsibility for the abuse without feeling the need to defend their family members.

Reinforcing survivors' perceptions of themselves as children when abused

Many of the cognitive procedures discussed above can be reinforced through the use of techniques that allow the client to consider more experientially their 'childlikeness' at the time of the abuse. Hall and Lloyd refer to this process as 're-entering the world of the child' (1989: 169).

For survivors, viewing photographs of themselves at the time of the abuse (considered earlier as a method to stimulate memory retrieval), and discussing their reactions to the photographs with a counselor or in a group setting, can reinforce the fact that the survivors were children at the time of the abuse, incapable of initiating or consenting to sexual activity (Cole and Barney, 1987; Hall and Lloyd, 1989). Family photographs further allow them to experience visually how small, and therefore dependent, they were, and how large, and therefore powerful, the offender was at the time of the abuse. Survivors can then often sympathize with the child in the photo, something they were unable to do for themselves.

Another technique that can serve a similar purpose is having survivors observe children who are close to the age of the survivors at the time of the abuse (Gordy, 1983). Visiting a nursery school class, for example, can be a powerful experience for survivors, enabling them to get in touch with their childhood needs and limitations. Some clinicians (Gordy, 1983) have suggested supplementing such activities with discussion of the stages of normal growth and development (e.g. according to Erikson, 1968) so that survivors can understand how the abuse interrupted their emotional growth as children.

Reinforcing reattribution of responsibility with other survivors

Bibliotherapy
Survivors can also profit from contact with other survivors as a way of reinforcing their reattributions of blame. By realizing how other survivors were engaged in the abuse, why they maintained their secret, and how they dealt with issues of responsibility, survivors can more easily come to accept that they were not responsible for their own abuse. One way of learning about the experiences of other survivors is by reading about their lives. This can initially be less threatening than speaking personally with other survivors and is often done by survivors prior to entering group counseling. Examples of books written about incest experiences include: *Daddy's girl* by Allen (1980); *I know why the caged bird sings* by Angelou (1971); *Kiss daddy goodnight* by Armstrong (1978); *I never told anyone: Writings by women survivors of child sexual abuse*, edited by Bass and Thornton (1983); *Father's days* by

Brady (1979); *Voices in the night: Women speaking about incest*, edited by McNaron and Morgan (1982); *Inside scars* by Sisk and Hoffman (1987); and *Men surviving incest* by Thomas (1989).

Group counseling

Another powerful reinforcement of new perceptions of the abuse experience is involvement in groups with other survivors of childhood sexual abuse. Group counseling as an adjunct treatment modality is discussed in detail later, but is mentioned here because one benefit of participating in a group is the power of other survivors to support the process of reattribution of blame. In groups, for example, survivors often find that the engagement and secrecy strategies (Sgroi and Bunk, 1988) used by their offenders and family were often similar to those used in other families. Gordy (1983) reported that members in her group identified a 'central motif,' which was that offenders frequently used brainwashing (e.g. convincing the child she had solicited the abuse) as a method of ensuring the child's silence and continued participation in the sexual abuse activities.

Discussing issues of responsibility, engagement processes, 'why me?' issues, and secret keeping within the group setting can be especially useful as survivors find they can appreciate that their peers were not to blame, had reasons for keeping the secret, and were powerless to stop the abuse. Because it is easier first to be 'objective' when evaluating the abuse situation of others, this process can reinforce survivors' developing beliefs about their own abuse. Tsai and Wagner reported that the following statement by a group leader can have a powerful effect on group members: 'Unless you can look at everyone else in this room and feel their guilt is warranted, your own guilt cannot be justified' (1978: 421).

Reaffirming new beliefs

The process of reframing the abuse experience, especially the re-attribution of blame, can be reinforced with techniques involving either vicarious or actual encounters with the offender or with important significant others. These techniques include role playing, letter writing, and actual confrontation.

Role playing

After survivors have worked on reframing the abuse from an adult perspective, emotionally and cognitively, it is helpful if they can assert their new beliefs experientially. For example, when the survivor has been able to reattribute the blame for the abuse to the offender, verbalizing this, even vicariously, to the offender or to important others can serve both to reaffirm the belief and to further integrate the affect associated with the belief.

Role playing may be done by using the Gestalt empty-chair technique in which the survivor is asked to 'imagine' the offender or other significant other sitting before them. Survivors can prepare a statement summarizing their new beliefs or discoveries, their feelings associated with these discoveries, and any questions they may have for the other individual before carrying out the role play. It is important for survivors to process their feelings and reactions to this experience as the role playing can be very powerful. For example, these role plays can often result in the release of a great deal of anger. Examples of role play scenarios may include:

- a female survivor telling her father that she now realized that as a 5-year-old child she was too young to initiate the abuse and therefore she was not a 'seductive little thing,' as he had always called her;
- a male survivor telling his uncle, the perpetrator, that although he did experience sexual arousal during the abusive experiences, he did not enjoy nor seek the sexual activity. The survivor expresses his anger toward the offender, reaffirms his sexual preference, and then tells his uncle that he (the survivor) no longer needs to hide his feelings behind a 'macho' image;
- a female survivor listing to her mother all the reasons she 'kept the secret' of her abuse by her father for so many years. She expresses disappointment that her mother was not 'strong enough' to hear that the abuse was occurring.

The following client–counselor interaction demonstrates how the counselor may facilitate the role play described in the first example. There is an empty chair that faces the client, Brenda. She has imagined that her father, whom she has not seen for many years, is in the chair. Brenda has made a list of things she would like to cover and has given this list to the counselor to help 'prompt' her.

Counselor: What would you like to tell your father?
Brenda: What a jerk he is.
Counselor: Why don't you tell him directly.
Brenda: OK. I think what you did to me when I was a little girl was horrible. It hurt me terribly. In fact, it really affected the rest of my life.
Counselor: Would you like to tell him how it hurt you?
Brenda: Yes. I grew up thinking I was to blame. You told me it happened because *I* was seductive. It started when I was only

5 years old. Ever since then I've thought all I was good for was sex.
I thought I was not good enough to have anyone love me.
Counselor: I know you also wanted to tell your dad what the abuse was
like for you when you were little.
Brenda: I was frightened to death. It hurt so much at first. I used to
pretend I wasn't there, like it was a dream. Once Mom took me to
the doctor for an infection. I felt so dirty. For years after I grew up
I could never go to the doctor. I've had so many medical problems.
Back then I prayed I would die. That's what you did to your little
5-year-old girl. [*Starts to cry*]
Counselor: You look at what happened differently now than you used
to. Tell your father what you've come to believe.
Brenda: I now believe that it was not my fault. It was entirely your
fault. You betrayed me. I did not know enough to be seductive at
first. I learned that from you and then that was the only way I knew
how to be with men. Now, I know I can be loved for *me*, as a person,
not because I'm 'sexy.' That was a line you fed me to keep me
involved with you.
Counselor: What else would you like to say to your father now?
Brenda: I don't wish you harm but neither do I forgive you. Mostly I
want you to know what you have done to me. You'll have to live with
that.

The counselor asked Brenda to take a few minutes at the end of
the role play to gather her thoughts. She and the counselor then
discussed what the experience was like for her. Brenda stated that
she began to feel very sad when discussing how she had felt as a
5-year-old. At this point in the role play, she re-experienced the
helplessness she had remembered from the childhood. However, by
telling her father her new beliefs, she was able to experience 'gaining control.' After the role play, Brenda identified her main feelings as sadness over the loss of her childhood, which her father had
taken from her. She did believe the role play helped her to reinforce her conviction that the abuse was not her fault.

Letter writing
A similar technique to reaffirm new beliefs is the use of the
'unsent' letter (Faria and Belohlavek, 1984; Hall and Lloyd, 1989;
Joy, 1987). Survivors write a letter to the offender or to others
with whom they wish to share their new beliefs regarding the
abuse. This technique is effective for survivors who find the empty-
chair technique too threatening or for survivors who find its
'dramatic' aspects too awkward. The letter remains unsent, as this
allows survivors to express their thoughts and feelings without
concern for the significant other's reaction. As with the role play,
it is important that the counselor process the experience with
survivors by exploring what it was like for them to write the letter

and what feelings were associated with the experience. (Actually mailing the letter involves some similar issues to confrontation, which is discussed below.) Survivors may wish to keep the letter in a safe place and add to it as they continue to develop new beliefs or experience new feelings. An example of an unsent letter from a male survivor to his abusive mother is included in Appendix A (p. 157).

Confrontation

Confronting the perpetrator can be a powerful opportunity for survivors to assert their new beliefs and perceptions of their abuse experience. However, confronting the perpetrator is an experience that has many ramifications for the healing process of survivors and should be processed thoroughly with them in counseling before the confrontation occurs (Agosta and Loring, 1988; Hall and Lloyd, 1989; Swanson and Biaggio, 1985).

Agosta and Loring (1988) have stressed that the decision to confront the perpetrator must originate with survivors themselves, since it is imperative that they perceive a confrontation as their choice. It is also important for survivors to realize that a confrontation with the offender is not a prerequisite to healing, rather it is an experience that can be very beneficial for some survivors. Because preparation is essential, it is helpful for the counselor to contract with survivors to engage in this preparation process before confronting the offender, as an impulsive confrontation can be harmful for survivors.

It is also important for the counselor to assess survivors' degree of readiness. Confrontation is most successful when survivors use the experience to assert, not to 'test out,' their new insights related to the sexual abuse experience. If survivors continue to struggle with denial, minimization, or self-blame (Hall and Lloyd, 1989), they are not ready to confront the offender, as the offender's response of denial, minimization, or blaming the survivor could be detrimental to the survivors' healing. One participant in the incest healing study (Draucker, 1992) gives an example of an unplanned, unsuccessful confrontation with her brother during a family reunion:

> Out of the blue I just said, '——, do you remember when we were eight – or when I was eight and you were eleven,' you know, and described the first incident of incest. He's like 'Well, yea, you know. I think I remember that.' And the way he was talking about it, it was like someone else had done it, not himself . . . and I kept asking more and more questions – just to verify that yes, at least it happened and I'm not crazy, you know, it did happen. And then I said, 'How do you feel

about that?' and he said, 'I don't feel responsible. My hormones were going crazy on me during adolescence and I had no control. I didn't know what I was doing.' . . . I said, 'I want you to say you're sorry.' He said, 'No, I'm not going to say I'm sorry because it's not my fault. I couldn't help myself.' And that was the end of that confrontation and that plummeted me down because OK, he's not going to take the blame for it, then it must have been my fault. So I took the blame and hated myself. So all last year I was really hating myself. That's what led to my intense misery.

Preparing for a confrontation involves an exploration of survivors' motivations, hopes, and desires. Many survivors may harbor the hope, even without realizing it, that the offender will admit to the abuse, fully recognize the impact it has had, and ask for forgiveness. If survivors can verbalize this hope, they often realize it is unrealistic and re-evaluate their need for the confrontation.

However, if survivors express the desire for a confrontation; have progressed significantly with issues of denial, minimization, and self-blame; and are not motivated by the hope of the offender's contrition, counselors may assist the survivor in preparing for a confrontation. Survivors must first decide how they would like to confront the offender (face to face, over the phone, by sending a letter). The pros and cons of each of these techniques can be discussed with survivors. Sending a letter may be less threatening, but may leave the survivor wondering if the letter was received and what the offender's response was to the letter. It is nonetheless often the method used when the survivor and the offender have been estranged for some time and the survivor does not desire personal contact. Confrontation over the phone can be less threatening than a face-to-face confrontation and would be safer if violence by the offender is a concern. However, the survivor is not privy to the offender's non-verbal responses and the offender can easily choose to hang up the phone at any time.

Face-to-face confrontations can be arranged in the presence of the counselor if the offender is willing to attend the survivor's counseling session. This usually occurs when the survivor continues to have a relationship with the offender and the offender has some investment in continuing to be involved in the survivor's life. In these cases, some survivors choose to make the offender's attendance at such a session a prerequisite for their continued relationship. If the survivor chooses a face-to-face confrontation with the offender outside of a counseling session, safety issues should be evaluated. It is helpful if the survivor has scheduled a counseling session shortly after the confrontation to discuss the experience with the counselor.

Prior to the confrontation, it is helpful if survivors plan, and perhaps role play, what they would like to say. In some cases the counselor may choose to help survivors with some basic communication 'tips' (e.g. the use of 'I' messages, ways to deal with manipulative communication). It is also helpful if survivors can predict the offender's possible responses. To facilitate this, counselors may ask what would be the offender's best, worst, and most likely reaction, and then assist survivors to plan their responses accordingly. It is helpful to remind survivors that, while they have experienced personal growth to get to this point, the offender probably has not and may well repeat behavior that is reminiscent of his or her behavior at the time of the abuse (e.g. denial, blaming).

It is also helpful for survivors to consider what feelings the confrontation experience might provoke. Survivors may need to provide for their self-care, safety, and self-nurturance needs in much the same way as they did following disclosure, as confrontation can evoke strong affective responses and at times a return of trauma symptomatology.

The same survivor discussed above described a more successful confrontation with her brother approximately a year after she had been in treatment:

> I was finally able to say, 'You screwed me up – it's your fault.' And that was a big deal for me to say. And I said, 'Consequently, I don't want you touching me ever, ever again. I don't want you to hug me when I come home. I don't want you to kiss me. I don't want to be your sister any more. I'm not hanging out with you any more . . . . Stay out of my way. I am going to get help because I like myself and I'm worth it . . . . You're the scumbag that did this to me and I'm going to reverse if it takes the rest of my life. But you're not going to beat me.' I go, 'I'm surviving. I'm a survivor.' And he was crying which was a big deal. . . . I don't care and I – it was a way of expressing myself and not really giving a s— what he had to say.

The process of confrontation may also be done with other significant family members. For example, some survivors may choose to confront a non-offending parent. This would also involve careful preparation and debriefing as it can be a powerful and threatening experience as well. This issue will be discussed later.

Case example

The following case exemplifies the process of reframing an experience of childhood sexual abuse from an adult perspective.

Eleanor was a 42-year-old successful businesswoman who sought counseling to deal with her experience of childhood sexual abuse after she had viewed a TV movie that dealt with incest. From the age of 8 to 13 she had been abused by her grandfather, who lived in her family's home. The abuse involved sexual fondling that usually occurred when Eleanor would come home from school and her parents were still at work. Although Eleanor described her adulthood as 'fairly normal,' she began to wonder following the movie if her avoidance of any intimate contact with men was related to her experience with her grandfather.

Eleanor made rapid progress in the early stages of counseling. She readily disclosed the abuse to her counselor and was able to describe the experience in detail. However, after approximately six months in counseling, Eleanor described feeling 'stuck' and wondered if she should discontinue treatment. When she introduced this concern, her counselor asked her what she hoped would happen next in the healing process. Eleanor discussed her belief that she was the cause of the abuse, that her grandfather was really just a 'lonely, pathetic man,' and that most of the fondling occurred because she would 'snuggle' next to him on the couch while they watched their afternoon TV shows. She claimed she had hoped that counseling would decrease her feelings of guilt, but, in fact, the more she discussed her experiences, the more she realized she wanted and sought her grandfather's attention. The following client–counselor interaction was aimed at reframing Eleanor's beliefs, related to responsibility for the abuse, from an adult perspective.

> *Eleanor:* I remember feeling miserable all day in school. I was lonely, didn't fit in with the other kids. Actually, I looked forward to coming home to be with Grandpa. He waited for me. I know this sounds stupid, but he always had milk and homemade cookies for me. We would have our afternoon shows. I would 'snuggle' with him on the couch and I liked that, so how can I say he abused me? I really did seek him out. He was just a poor old man. I cannot blame him for what happened. If I had been out playing like normal kids, none of this would have happened.
>
> *Counselor:* Tell me more about the loneliness you felt as an 8-year-old.
>
> *Eleanor:* Well, up until that time we moved a lot. My father did a residency in Chicago; then my mother did hers in Boston. Then back to Chicago, where my father did some research. You get the picture . . . . Anyway, I was never in one place very long and my parents were always at the hospital or the lab. I spent a lot of time with relatives. I think my mother really resented Grandpa needing to move in with us because now she had two of us to take care of. I think she regretted having me, interfered with her work, you know. No, I shouldn't say this. They were OK parents. Now my mother is kind

of famous. She was just sort of cold and distant. I never remember either of them playing with me. It didn't help that I was so shy. I guess it's natural that Grandpa and I hooked up. God, I sound like a whiner, don't I?

Counselor: No. You sound like someone describing a childhood during which you were uprooted a lot, you didn't feel wanted or attended to, and you experienced a lot of loneliness. You were missing the attention, and the affection, you needed. When your grandfather came along and provided those things for you, that naturally felt good.

Eleanor: Yes, it did feel good.

Counselor: It sounds like, at that time in your life, your grandfather was the only one available to provide those things. All 8-year-olds need attention and affection.

Eleanor: Yes, so do forty-somethings. [*Laughs*]

Counselor: How true!

Eleanor: Attention and affection were certainly things my parents did not provide. They gave me everything else. Everything else materialistic that is. But I knew that along with the attention from my grandfather was the sex. I always knew that.

Counselor: It sounds like you were needing your grandfather's attention and his affection when you 'sought him out.' Because you could not get those things from others in your life, you sought them from the only adult who was available. It was natural for you to do this as a child. Any lonely 8-year-old would have done the same thing. Seeking attention and affection is very different than seeking, or being responsible for, sexual abuse.

Eleanor: Yes, I guess I really did need him for those other things.

Counselor: As a child everything probably seemed confusing to you. You needed your grandfather's affection, but along with that, he used you sexually. As an adult you can appreciate that you were naturally seeking to meet your needs for attention and affection, but you were not seeking the sexual abuse nor were you responsible for it.

Eleanor: Yes, that is true. The sex part I hated.

In this interaction, the counselor explored with Eleanor what she had needed as an 8-year-old child and challenged the belief that because Eleanor was desperate for her grandfather's affection, she also desired, and was therefore responsible for, the sexual abuse. The counselor and Eleanor had several similar interactions to reinforce this belief as Eleanor had been convinced for many years that she had sought the sexual activity.

Eleanor was able to express anger and disappointment toward her 'absentee' parents, but actually attributing the blame for the abuse to her grandfather was very difficult and occurred only after the counselor encouraged Eleanor to discuss the positive memories she had of him. When she could acknowledge that her grandfather was not a 'horrible monster,' she could also acknowledge that he engaged in the sexual activity to meet his own needs. Eleanor struggled for some time before accepting that she could be angry about the abuse without discounting the positive feelings she had had toward her grandfather. The following interaction between her and the counselor represents the point in the counseling process when she did begin to accept her grandfather's responsibility for the abuse.

> *Eleanor:* He was really sweet and kind in many ways. Why he did what he did I will never know. He must not have known how much it hurt me.
>
> *Counselor:* As children, we usually assume that adults are all good or all bad. Because your grandfather was kind and attentive, and because you really appreciated much of your time together, you assumed he was all good. Unfortunately, that led you to believe you were bad. As adults, we can appreciate that people have good and bad points and do good and bad things. Your grandfather is no exception. He was kind and gentle and attentive and he also used you as a little girl to meet his own needs.
>
> *Eleanor:* Yes, he did do that. And because of that I do feel betrayed by him. If he was sick, he should have gotten help. What he did has caused me grief my whole life. Sometimes I do feel angry about that. Yet, I still miss him. That does not make sense.
>
> *Counselor:* Maybe it does. You loved him and would naturally miss him. But you can also feel angry and betrayed as well.

Eleanor also struggled with the fact that the abuse had lasted for a long time, past when she 'should have known better.' Again, by reviewing her emotionally unmet needs, she was able to state that she needed attention and affection as much at the age of 13 as she did when she was 8. Eleanor was quite clear that she did not tell her parents of the abuse because they would have 'kicked' her grandfather out of the house, a prospect she could not tolerate.

Although she decided not to disclose the abuse to her parents, Eleanor identified the need to get some 'closure' on her relationship with her grandfather, who was now dead. She visited his grave, which was in another state, and told him how she had been hurt by the abuse. She explained to him that she could not forgive him, but that she was grateful for the non-sexual activities they shared and for the attention he gave her. She told him that her sense of betrayal, rather than anger, was now paramount.

There were several aspects of Eleanor's abuse experience that made the reframing process challenging. Reattribution of blame was especially difficult because, in many ways, her grandfather had been her main source of emotional support as a child. For this reason, it was especially important that the counselor respected the loyalty (Gelinas, 1983) that Eleanor felt toward her grandfather. Because she did not need to defend him, Eleanor could hold her grandfather, rather than herself, responsible for the abuse. A key issue that Eleanor needed to explore was the emotional void she experienced as a child, so that she could see that although she would seek out her grandfather, she craved his affection, a basic childhood need, not the sexual activity. A counseling intervention that would encourage Eleanor to explore what an average 8-year-old would know about sex might have further reinforced for Eleanor that her needs were emotional, not sexual, and that as a child she would have trouble differentiating affectionate touches from sexual touches.

Although Eleanor responded well to cognitive challenges, the experiential part of her healing seemed to come when she visited her grandfather's grave. The counselor's role in this process was to assist Eleanor in planning what she wanted to say, in anticipating what her emotional response might be, and in planning for ways to care for herself following the experience. The counselor and Eleanor had several 'debriefing' sessions following Eleanor's graveside visit.

5
Addressing the Context of the Sexual Abuse

As survivors examine the sexual abuse experience from an adult perspective and some of the guilt and shame they have struggled with begins to dissipate, there are several other issues that are important to address in counseling. As the sexual abuse did not occur in a vacuum, exploration of other relevant issues that had an impact on childhood development can enhance the ongoing process of connecting developmental influences with current concerns. This chapter will address the processes of exploring the context of the abuse, exploring the role of non-offending family members and connecting these early experiences with specific current concerns.

Exploring the context of the abuse

Although the focus on the sexual abuse experience itself is an important counseling intervention, it is essential to acknowledge that sexual abuse occurs within a larger context, often within a family system. Other significant factors that had an impact on the survivor's development therefore need to be addressed and explored. These have been called the 'life context of the sexual abuse' (Sgroi and Bunk, 1988: 148). Addressing other experiences and relationships, both positive and negative, aids survivors to avoid the conclusion that their development was shaped entirely by their abuse. As Davis states:

> For some survivors it [the sexual abuse] is by far the most pervasive influence. For others, growing up in a racist society, being adopted, living in poverty, or being the first child of five had an equal or greater impact. In assessing its effects on your life, it's important to put the abuse in perspective with the other forces that shaped you. (1990: 138–9)

One survivor in the incest healing study (Draucker, 1992), stressed the importance of dealing with other contextual issues:

> I think what the incest survivors' group did for me was have a . . . it was a forum for all of us to explore whatever those childhood issues were. It wasn't just the incest, but as soon as I say that, for me what comes up are the abandonment issues.

Significant childhood influences are of course numerous and varied. Important factors to explore include family composition (e.g. the loss of a parent through divorce, death, separation; the role of other significant caretakers; the survivor's birth order; the number of siblings in the family), social factors (e.g. ethnic origin, socioeconomic class, religious influences), other significant family pathology or stressors (e.g. parental alcoholism, emotional or physical abuse, mental illness, criminal behavior), and extra-familial resources (e.g. relationships with teachers, sports activities, counseling involvement).

Exploring family functioning
Recently, the concept of adult children of dysfunctional families has been applied to individuals from families with diverse problems (e.g. alcoholism, sexual abuse, physical abuse, emotional neglect), as these individuals often struggle with similar concerns. For example, there are significant parallels between Gelinas' (1983) description of the parentified child in the incestuous family and Wegscheider-Cruse's (1985) description of the family hero in the chemically dependent family (i.e. a family in which at least one member abuses drugs or alcohol). The family hero is the child who assumes responsibility for other family members and contributes to the family's public presentation of normality through his or her good behavior and achievements. Both parentified children and family heroes assume adult responsibilities and learn to meet the needs of others while denying their own needs, often losing the opportunity for a normal childhood. Other roles identified by Wegscheider-Cruse (1985) include the enabler, who supports the behavior of the chemically dependent person by attempting to help or 'cover' for him or her; the family scapegoat, who draws attention away from the family's problems by 'getting into trouble' (e.g. at school, with the law); the lost child, who 'quietly' withdraws from the family; and the mascot, who draws attention away from the family's problems by providing humor and mischief.

Satir (1988) compared the closed system of 'troubled' families and the open system of 'nurturing' families. In a closed family system, communication is indirect, unclear, and non-specific; rules are inflexible and covert; and self-esteem among members is low. In an open family system, communication is direct, clear, and specific; rules are flexible and overt; and self-esteem among members is high. In a closed system, outside influences are discouraged, whereas in an open system free exchange with the environment is sought. Closed family systems are dysfunctional because they prohibit the growth potential of their members.

Farmer has identified eight 'specific interactional elements' (1989: 18) that are characteristic of abusive families. These elements are denial, inconsistency and unpredictability, lack of empathy, lack of clear boundaries, role reversal, the closed family system, incongruent communication, and too much or too little conflict. Farmer has also identified the general effects exhibited by adults who have grown up in abusive families. These include lack of trust, avoidance of feelings, low self-esteem, a sense of helplessness, and difficulty in relationships.

A concept that has emerged from the literature on adult children of dysfunctional families is that of 'healing the child within' (Whitfield, 1989). Whitfield defined the child within as 'the part of each of us which is ultimately alive, energetic, creative, and fulfilled; it is our Real Self – who we truly are' (1989: 1). Due to certain childhood experiences such as emotional neglect, alcoholism, or abuse individuals learn to deny their child within. This results in passivity; self-criticism; orientation toward others; and inhibition of creativity, spontaneity, and joy in adulthood. Counseling procedures have been recommended based on the concept of the child within, sometimes referred to as the inner child. Farmer (1989), for example, discussed techniques for reparenting the inner child using imagery. This involves first 'releasing' one's original parents by recognizing that they are the products of their 'own fragmented, injurious childhoods' (1989: 104) and by accepting that one no longer requires anything from one's parents to survive. Creating new internal parents is accomplished by imaging a mother and father (i.e. a 'Good Mother' and a 'Good Father') who possess desired parental qualities, such as protectiveness, supportiveness, and sensitivity. Finally, adopting one's inner child involves first imaging a time from one's childhood when one was hurt and then imaging a 'Good Mother' or a 'Good Father' showing concern and caring for one's needs. Farmer suggests that through this activity one can learn to provide nurturance for one's own inner child.

Characteristics of dysfunctional families often provide the context of the sexual abuse experience. Healing is facilitated if survivors are able to focus on the sexual abuse experience itself and to place it in the larger perspective of their overall childhood development. For example, counselors may ask clients to consider Farmer's eight elements of abusive families or the roles of a dysfunctional family as suggested by Wegscheider-Cruse and reflect on those issues that were salient in their own families of origin. Survivors may then reflect on issues such as how incongruent communication in their family of origin has had an impact on their current communication patterns or how their role as the family hero continues to be carried out in their present lives. It is also useful if survivors are encouraged to discuss the influence of positive childhood factors, whether intra-familial or extra-familial, on their present development.

Case vignette

The following case vignette, an interaction between a survivor and her counselor, highlights the importance of exploring the context of the abuse in order for survivors to be able to place their sexual abuse experience in a meaningful context. Heather, a 24-year-old graduate student, had been sexually abused by an uncle on several occasions when she was 12 years old. She had sought counseling originally to deal with frequent nightmares and several phobias (e.g. being alone in the dark, taking showers when alone in her apartment). After focusing on the abuse experience, her symptoms essentially subsided. Yet Heather complained that she still felt that there were pieces of the experience with which she had not come to terms. After several sessions spent exploring what was 'missing' for her, Heather decided to explore more closely the dynamics of her family of origin. She had claimed they were a normal, very close, family. Her mother and father had maintained that the abusive uncle was truly a black sheep in an otherwise very respectable extended family. Her father had banned the uncle from any further contact with Heather's family when she told her father that the uncle had molested her. However, upon exploring some of her family's responses to the abuse more closely, and identifying some family dysfunction, Heather was better able to understand both her response to the abuse and her ways of coping with problems more generally.

Heather: It was weird. They [her parents] were very supportive. They told me it was not my fault, that I shouldn't worry about it. My father told my uncle never to see me or any of the family again. They even took me on a wonderful trip to help me get over it. In fact, at the time I thought it brought us closer together.
Counselor: Looking back now, what about that seemed weird?
Heather: Well, I guess that when we got back from the trip no more was said. I mean, they were still supportive. When I would dream about my uncle, my mother would come into my room, get me water, rub my back, generally calm me down. But she would never ask what the dream was about. I assumed she did not want to bring up bad memories.
Counselor: And what do you think now?
Heather: Well now I realize I needed to talk about it. Also, I guess I wonder why they never brought charges against him or got me any

professional help. In those days I guess people did not do that as much. But I still wonder why they didn't. What if he did the same thing to one of my cousins?

Counselor: What does their response tell you about your family?

Heather: I think that they tried very hard to be the perfect family. We never fought, never got angry at each other. Appearance was important to the outside world. Because of this, I think, the abuse was denied, swept under the rug, maybe. They told me it was not my fault, for which I am really grateful, but we never talked any more about it again. They should have at least told my other uncles and aunts to watch out for their kids. I guess by not acknowledging it to the outside world, we could keep our image of the normal family. But, you know, it was not just the abuse. For example, my mother had breast cancer when I was young and never told anyone, not even me, until years later. She quit her job as a schoolteacher rather than tell anyone she had cancer.

Counselor: How did your family's way of handling the abuse affect your healing?

Heather: It fed into my denial, I think. Made the abuse seem more unreal. Like it never happened. More importantly, I guess, I learned not to face things myself. Do you know I've had a lump in my breast for six months and I've not had it checked out.

Exploring her family's functioning, both in response to the abuse and more generally, allowed Heather to gain insight into some of her present experiences. Although the trauma symptomatology did seem to result directly from her abuse, other issues she faced (such as her tendency to 'avoid' problems) were related to other family and developmental influences as well. Until these issues were addressed, she had felt something was missing from her healing experiences.

Exploring the role of the non-offending family members

Another context issue is the role of important non-offending family members in the abuse. While survivors often struggle with their feelings toward the offender, a potentially potent issue is their feelings toward other family members who were present when the abuse occurred. As the most frequently described incidents of abuse involve adult male offenders, often fathers or stepfathers, and female child victims, the non-offending family member most often addressed in the literature is the mother.

Historically, mothers have often been 'blamed' for the abuse that occurs in the family. In both popular and clinical literature it has been suggested that the cold, sexually unavailable wife drove her husband to her daughter and at times colluded in the abuse to avoid her own marital, sexual 'responsibilities.' The offender is therefore thought to hold no responsibility for the abuse. In reaction to this sexist attitude, some counselors have discouraged survivors from exploring their feelings toward their mothers. Herman for example, critiqued a treatment program that prohibits 'mother-blaming' by survivors:

> Although fathers and not mothers are entirely to blame, victims must be permitted to express the depth of their anger at both parents. The victim who is not permitted to express her anger at her mother or her tender feelings for her father will not be able to transcend these feelings or to put them in a new perspective. (1981: 200)

In addressing reactions toward the non-offending family member it is important for both counselors and survivors to differentiate responsibility for protecting the child and responsibility for the abuse itself (Hall and Lloyd, 1989). As Gelinas (1983) stated, the abuser is always responsible for the sexual contact, whereas all adult family members are responsible for the incestuous family dynamics.

The non-offending family member could be any responsible older person or caretaker in the family when the abuse occurred. However, survivors usually struggle with issues related to a parent or parents who did not protect them, so non-offending parents will be the focus of this discussion.

Inevitably, survivors will explore the role of non-offending parents in the abuse and the counselor may facilitate this exploration. There are several possibilities regarding the role of non-offending parents: they had no knowledge of the abuse; they suspected but did not acknowledge the abuse; they knew of the abuse but did not intervene; or they knew of the abuse and condoned it (Hall and Lloyd, 1989). Although survivors may never definitely know which role a non-offending parent played, many survivors, after exploring the possibilities and confronting their own denial and minimization, usually come to some conclusion about this issue.

Determining the role of a non-offending parent can be a difficult process. Some survivors state that it is easier to hate the offender than to be angry at their mother, whom they may still love and with whom they may have close, current contact. As one survivor in the incest healing study (Draucker, 1992) stated:

> But my stepfather, I don't care about. I was more hurt by my mom staying with him. I couldn't care less. I don't care if I ever see him again. I just don't like him as a person. . . . but my mom hurt me more because I care about her more. Do you see that?

Therefore, it is important for counselors to encourage survivors to express their feelings about non-offending parents. These feelings may range from disappointment that a parent was not strong enough to recognize the abuse to intense rage because a parent knew of the abuse and either ignored it or condoned it.

Hall and Lloyd (1989) have also suggested that it can be helpful if survivors explore the reasons for the actions of the non-offending parents and place their behavior in the larger context of the dynamics of the family. Encouraging such an exploration should not imply that survivors are not entitled to their angry feelings or that they should forgive the non-offending parent for their actions. Rather, this process may assist survivors to make sense of their own experience. For example, it could be helpful for a survivor to understand her non-offending mother's family history, which may have included childhood abuse, and to recognize her mother's conviction that she could not survive independently from her abusive husband. These factors provide some explanation for the mother's inactivity and inability to protect her child.

In some cases, survivors may choose to be seen in counseling with a non-offending parent. This is usually most successful when survivors have worked through some basic issues (e.g. denial, minimization) and now desire a better understanding of the family's issues at the time of the abuse. As with a confrontation with the offender, joint work with a survivor and a non-offending parent takes preparation by both parties (exploration of motivations for the joint sessions, risks involved, and so on). For example, each party needs to reflect whether the goal of the joint session is confrontation, providing an explanation of the abuse context, or actually repairing the current relationship between survivor and non-offending parent. In some instances it is helpful if a non-offending parent is assigned his or her own counselor, either to deal with the personal issues that might arise from the joint sessions or to provide support within the joint sessions themselves. In some cases, non-offending parents may experience a crisis when confronted about their role in the abuse, as they may well have denied or minimized the event in much the same way as the survivor did. They therefore may need additional therapeutic services.

In the following client–counselor interaction, Patricia, a 23-year-old woman, prepares to invite her mother, a non-offending parent, to a counseling session. Prior to this interaction, Patricia and the counselor had explored Patricia's assumptions and conclusions about her mother's knowledge of the sexual abuse of Patricia by Patricia's older brother. Having concluded that her mother knew of the abuse 'on some level,' Patricia had discussed her feelings (e.g. anger, betrayal) regarding this conclusion in counseling. While she was addressing her mother's role in the family's abuse dynamics, Patricia had limited the contact she had with her. However, as she had always felt close to her mother, Patricia decided to invite her to a session with the hopes of re-establishing their relationship. In the following interaction, Patricia began to determine her goals, hopes, and expectations for this session.

Patricia: How could he [her brother] do this to me for so many years and her not know it? I mean, maybe she knew, but really didn't want to know. We'll see what she says when she's in here.

Counselor: When your mom comes to the session, what would you like to have happen?

Patricia: Part of me hopes she's totally shocked when I tell her. You know, that she had no idea and that she wants to kill him now. Then we can get on with our relationship. [*Pauses*] Even if that does happen, I guess I still know she knew, somehow. Maybe unconsciously.

Counselor: If the session confirms for you what you suspect, what might that be like for you?

Patricia: I thought I'd be devastated to find out she knew but I guess now I just need to ask so I can move on. I probably also want some kind of apology, I guess. I guess I want more to know why she didn't stop it. She's always been a wimp – especially towards my dad. But if she loved me enough, she would have done something. [*Starts to cry*] In answer to your question, I guess I won't be devastated really, but I will feel hurt.

Counselor: Regardless of how consciously or unconsciously your mom was aware of the abuse, it hurts to realize she did not protect you.

Patricia: Yes, and made no attempt to do so. I just wish she were stronger. I don't want to cut her out of my life but I can't go on pretending nothing happened.

Counselor: There are several things you've said you would like to accomplish with your mom. Getting the abuse out in the open, an apology perhaps, and an explanation for why she did not stop the abuse. Ultimately, if possible, I know you would like to resume your relationship. When we meet next week, which of these goals would you like to focus on? We can then see if your mom agrees to the same goal.

Patricia: Basically, to get the abuse out in the open and to ask her why she did not protect me.

Counselor: How might she respond when you ask why?

Patricia: Well, she might say she doesn't know the answer to why.

Counselor: What would that be like for you?

Patricia: I think it would be OK. As long as she agrees to talk about it.

Counselor: And if she will not talk about it?

Patricia: I'd be angry but at least I would know what she is willing to do.

Connecting present concerns with childhood experiences

Addressing abuse context issues will facilitate survivors' ability to connect their childhood experiences with their current issues. Although a general acceptance by survivors that their present concerns are related to their sexual abuse experiences must often occur prior to their contracting to focus on the abuse, actually making and understanding the connections is a process that occurs throughout much of counseling. While survivors may have considered that their present difficulties may reflect coping mechanisms that they used as children to adapt to the abuse, it is only when they make concrete connections between their present-day experiences and their childhood experiences that they can begin to perceive themselves as survivors rather than victims. This process is enhanced if the counselor encourages survivors to fully describe their current experiences (e.g. incidents that occurred between sessions) and then asks the survivors to consider how their handling of these situations may be related to the survival skills they learned as an abused child.

One participant in the incest healing study (Draucker, 1992) described this process in her own therapy:

> I think then probably what she [her therapist] did for me, or what we worked on together, was to talk about what had happened and for her to help me see how as a child, you start doing things to cope and to get by. And then what she did was bring it into the present day. It seemed like she had a very good ability to – you know, I would come in and start to talk about some problems that I was having today whether it was with my family or my boss or ____ who is my husband, and in the next few sessions we would get back into the abuse time period and she would help me see how the way I reacted to that was affecting the way I react to people today.

Often, survivors respond to the counselor as they did to significant individuals from their past, so it is important that survivors are able to connect their present reactions toward the counselor with the abuse experience. They may expect that the counselor will hurt them through rejection, exploitation, or manipulation and respond to the counselor with fear, mistrust, rage, or excessive dependency. Counselors must address these issues with survivors to help them connect their current reactions with the abuse. Counselors must also avoid an authoritarian approach, set clear and realistic limits, and reinforce survivors' independence and self-acceptance (Briere and Runtz, 1988).

Case study

The following case shows the importance of addressing the context
of a sexual abuse experience in counseling. Jerry was a 36-year-old
married male who worked with his father in a small family-owned
machine shop. He sought counseling at a community mental health
center because he had a depression that he could 'not shake.' Jerry
claimed that he was tired most of the time, could not concentrate
on his work, and had lost all sexual desire. Although he claimed
his relationship with his wife of eight years had always been good,
he also indicated that they were currently experiencing some
problems because they could not conceive a child and, after years
of infertility treatment, had 'given up.' Jerry stated that he was
content not to have children, but had problems dealing with his
wife's disappointment. He reported that she frequently complained
that he was unavailable to her emotionally and that she felt like she
was dealing with this loss 'all alone.'

Jerry was the youngest of three children. His older brother,
Tom, aged 44, was an alcoholic who worked sporadically at the
machine shop. His older sister, Jean, aged 40, was the office
manager at the shop. Jerry stated that she was the one who 'kept
things going.' Jean was married with two children. Jerry stated
that his father was an alcoholic who nonetheless managed to show
up at the shop 'every day for 35 years.' His mother stayed at home
and was always 'pretty unhappy.'

When asked about significant childhood events, Jerry reluctantly
revealed that at the age of 11 he had been molested in the park on
his way home from school by two older boys whom he knew. They
asked him to play a 'game' with them that resulted in each of them
penetrating Jerry anally. Jerry was upset by the experience and told
Tom that it had occurred. His brother responded by saying it
'sounded like fun' and then molested Jerry himself. This abuse by
Tom, involving anal intercourse, occurred several more times. Tom
threatened that if Jerry told their parents of their activities, Tom
would deny it and would beat Jerry for telling. Apparently, Tom
had been physically violent when the brothers were younger.

The initial focus of counseling was on the abuse experience itself.
Jerry dealt with issues of self-blame for not standing up to his
brother and the other boys, anger toward Tom, and questions
regarding his own sexuality. However, much of Jerry's counseling
also involved addressing the context of the sexual abuse. Jerry was
encouraged by the counselor to describe his family members, their
relationships with each other, and major family events. In the
following interaction, the counselor introduces the idea that

experiences that accompanied the abuse could have had an important impact on Jerry's development.

> *Counselor:* Jerry, you've worked hard dealing with your abuse experiences and the impact they've had on your life. I also wonder about other things that were occurring in your family at that time.
> *Jerry:* I'm not sure what you mean.
> *Counselor:* Sometimes other things that children experience – such as with family members other than the offender – can affect them in adulthood. For example, I wonder what your relationship with your parents was like at that time . . . .
> *Jerry:* Well, it was not good with my dad. I guess you could say he was drunk . . . .

The family did have many attributes of a dysfunctional family. Jerry's dad was clearly an alcoholic and his mother was apparently chronically depressed. Jerry stated that his father drank 8–10 beers nightly until he passed out, although he never missed work. His mother would complain about his father's drinking and would 'cry a lot.' Jerry also remembered that she was always extremely tired. He recalled her telling business associates who called when his father was drunk that he was not at home. She would also keep the children quiet so as not to disturb him, as he would get quite irritable when drinking. Jean, as a child, did well in school and was actively involved in the family business at a young age. The family was 'shocked' when she got pregnant and married at the age of 16, because she had always been 'so good.' Tom, as a child, was always in trouble at school and had several minor scraps with the law for various violations (e.g. petty theft, disturbing the peace). Jerry described Tom as a bully who never obeyed their parents. On the other hand, Jerry described himself as a loner in school who never caused the family any trouble. He stated that his family 'kind of ignored me.' He worked in the machine shop as a boy but never enjoyed his work.

In counseling, Jerry did some reading on dysfunctional chemically dependent families and became animated when discussing how 'classically' his family members played the 'roles.' His mother's enabling behaviors were clear and he remarked that Tom played the 'scapegoat'; Jean, the 'hero'; and himself the 'lost child.' Having this understanding of his family was seemingly helpful to Jerry in accepting that he wasn't just a 'loser.' He recognized that his family's poor communication styles and isolation from the community, except through the business, were also characteristics of a dysfunctional family.

However, the process of dealing with his feelings toward his 'non-offending' parents regarding the sexual abuse was a more difficult process for Jerry. He stated that he had never considered that they ever knew of the abuse, but had begun to question why this was so. It was only after being in counseling for almost a year that he did begin to express disappointment and anger that his parents were unable to protect him from the abuse. He recognized that he never told them of the abuse because he believed they could not have helped him. The following interaction represents Jerry's struggle with this issue.

Jerry: I guess I always knew they [his parents] had problems of their own but I never thought their problems affected me – or had anything to do with what my brother did to me. But maybe, I don't know, if they had not been messed up. I never told them though.

Counselor: Remember yourself as a young boy. Why might you not have told them?

Jerry: Well, I probably knew they couldn't – or wouldn't – do anything to stop Tom. He ran wild. They couldn't control him.

Counselor: So you probably felt that telling them would be futile.

Jerry: Yes. When I talk about them they sound like losers. Now I guess I do wish they did something. Ya – I guess some parents might have done something, or noticed something happening, or found out. I wish mine had. I sure wish they stopped it. [*Speaks softly, begins to fidget*] It's Tom's doing though, not theirs.

Counselor: Yes, only Tom is responsible for abusing you and I know you've expressed the rage and hurt you feel toward him. It seems hard however for you to discuss your disappointment that your parents did not take action to stop him somehow.

Jerry: Ya, I'm not sure why.

Jerry was able to connect his current concerns with the abuse situation in several ways. He recognized that he was dealing with the pain of infertility by withdrawing from his wife, much as he had withdrawn from his dysfunctional family to try to avoid pain. He had attributed the infertility problems to himself, although the couple had been given a diagnosis of idiopathic, or unexplained, infertility. Jerry knew that as an adolescent he had extreme concerns that he was gay and realized that currently, on some level, he thought the infertility reflected his lack of manliness. Just as he blamed himself for not protecting himself from his brother's abuse by concluding he was not a 'man,' he blamed himself for the infertility by deciding that, regardless of what the doctors said, he was sterile. This served to reinforce his already poor self-concept.

Jerry's healing involved dealing both with the abuse experience itself and with the context within which it occurred. He recognized that as a result of being the 'lost' child in his dysfunctional family he felt insignificant and was left without the emotional resources to deal with his current crisis. He had learned to unjustly blame himself for the abuse, and also blamed himself unjustly for the infertility. Once he addressed these misperceptions, he could give up the view of himself as 'unmanly' and begin to make changes in his life. These changes will be discussed in the following chapter.

6
Making Desired Life Changes

Once survivors have addressed issues related to the sexual abuse experience and its context, and have connected their childhood coping patterns with their current concerns, they are able to begin to make desired life changes. This chapter will address some of the behavioral and lifestyle changes frequently made by survivors.

Dealing with current concerns

An important phase of the healing process occurs when survivors explore which aspects of their lives have been particularly affected by the abuse. They may then begin to make the life changes they desire. Three areas of adult adjustment that are often addressed in counseling with survivors are self-esteem, interpersonal functioning, and sexual functioning.

Self-esteem
Self-esteem is one of the major personal issues that survivors struggle with throughout the healing process. Although the reframing of the abuse experience (as previously discussed) can be effective in addressing the guilt and shame that underlies the survivors' negative self-image, dealing with self-esteem often remains a salient issue. Negative self-concept related to self-blame for the abuse is typically generalized to other areas of survivors' functioning.

Addressing self-esteem is frequently identified as a counseling goal, but it is sometimes approached in an oversimplified manner (e.g. giving a client 'positive feedback'). Peplau has proposed a model that can guide the counselor in addressing self-esteem issues in an in-depth manner (O'Toole and Welt, 1989). This model suggests that there are three dimensions, or self-views, that comprise one's concept of the self. The first dimension, the 'self-views in awareness,' consists of conscious, familiar, and often articulated self-perceptions. These views reflect the messages about oneself that were heard frequently from significant others in childhood. The 'self-views in awareness' of survivors of childhood sexual abuse are often that they are bad, worthless, or dirty.

The second dimension, the 'maybe me self-views,' consists of self-perceptions that are not immediately in one's awareness. However, one may apply these views to oneself if one's attention is directed toward them. These views reflect infrequently heard messages in childhood. For survivors of abuse, the 'maybe me self-views' are often positive qualities that perhaps teachers or other adults had pointed out. The 'maybe me self-view' might be that the survivor was a good student and a child of some worth to someone.

The third dimension, the 'not me self-views,' consists of self-perceptions that are out of awareness. Because these views are associated with severe anxiety, they are dissociated from the individual's experience. The 'not me self-views' for survivors of abuse are often that they are worthy, valuable individuals who possess basic personal rights. Although these are positive qualities, such self-views are at odds with the ways in which survivors are accustomed to perceiving themselves.

Counseling interventions Often, survivors make negative comments about themselves reflecting their low self-esteem and requiring intervention by counselors. Peplau cautioned counselors against challenging these negative 'self-views in awareness' with laudatory comments regarding clients' value or worth in order to improve their self-esteem (O'Toole and Welt, 1989). 'Self-views in awareness,' although negative, are comfortable and expected. Compliments regarding the positive qualities of clients often reflect their 'not me self-views' and are therefore associated with anxiety and result in defensiveness. Instead of praising clients, counselors should first facilitate discussion of ways in which a 'self-view in awareness' was noticed by the client or stated by others. Peplau called this method an investigative approach. A client statement exemplifying a negative 'self-view in awareness' and non-facilitative and facilitative counselor responses are outlined in Table 6.1.

Peplau believes that through this type of discussion, 'maybe me' statements will emerge (O'Toole and Welt, 1989). A 'maybe me' statement is often a tentative or conditional positive self-statement. The counselor can reinforce this statement with specific observations and have clients describe situations in which they have experienced the 'maybe me self-view.' A client statement exemplifying a 'maybe me self-view' and non-facilitative and facilitative counselor responses are outlined in Table 6.2.

Table 6.1 *Interventions for statements reflecting the 'self-view in awareness'*

Client statement:	I am a slut. I'm not worth you helping me.
Non-facilitative counselor response:	I think you are a worthwhile person and I look forward to helping you.
Facilitative counselor responses:	1 Tell me who first told you that you were a slut. (Exploring when self-view was *said*)
	2 When did you first feel worthless? (Exploring when self-view was *noticed*)
	3 Tell me about a specific time that you felt like a slut. (Exploring when self-view was *applied*)

Table 6.2 *Interventions for statements reflecting the 'maybe me self-view'*

Client statement:	Well, I guess not everyone thinks of me as a slut just because that's what my stepfather told me I was. The other group members don't seem to look at me like this.
Non-facilitative counselor response:	Yes, they see you for the worthwhile human being you are.
Facilitative counselor responses:	1 Yes, I've noticed they have commented that you have useful things to say. (Feedback-specific observation)
	2 Yes, I've noticed others in the group do treat you with respect. (Feedback-specific observation)
	3 Tell me about other people who do not consider you a slut. (Exploring when self-view is experienced)

Peplau emphasized that when clients begin to express positive 'not me self-views,' it is important for the counselor to address the anxiety that is likely to be associated with these views (O'Toole and Welt, 1989). Clients can be encouraged to describe feelings related to a self-view that is at variance with the self-view to which they are accustomed and to begin to consider how this new self-view can be applied. A client statement exemplifying a 'not me self-view'

Table 6.3   *Interventions for statements reflecting the 'not me self-view'*

Client statement:	I realize now that I am not a slut. I am a worthwhile human being.
Non-facilitative counselor response:	I'm glad you've realized this. It will make a big difference in your life. I'm very happy for you.
Facilitative counselor responses:	1 What is it like for you to think of yourself in this new way? (Exploring feelings) 2 Tell me about a situation in which you have (or will) apply this new way of looking at yourself. (Exploring ways to apply this self-view)

and non-facilitative and facilitative counselor responses are outlined in Table 6.3.

Peplau's model therefore suggests that constructive, positive self-views emerge only after the more familiar self-views are processed and only if the anxiety generated by the positive self-views is acknowledged and addressed (O'Toole and Welt, 1989). Positive self-views often do not emerge until late in counseling.

Interpersonal functioning

As the self-esteem of survivors begins to improve, an important issue becomes making changes in their current relationships. Interpersonal problems of survivors range from social isolation to involvement in relationships that are destructive or abusive. Because sexual abuse involves a disregard for the physical and emotional boundaries of children, typically by a supposedly trustworthy other, important relationship issues for survivors are establishing boundaries between themselves and others and developing trust.

Counselors may assist survivors in evaluating their current relationships by exploring how these relationships meet the survivors' needs for independence, as well as for intimacy, and how the relationships enhance or detract from the survivors' growth and healing. Making connections between present relationships and their abuse experience can facilitate this process. Survivors often discover, for example, that they are unable to express anger in their current relationships because they learned in childhood that expression of anger resulted in negative consequences (e.g. a beating, further sexual abuse, rejection).

Establishing boundaries The healing process for survivors often involves learning to establish personal boundaries. In the abuse situation, survivors were frequently part of an enmeshed family system in which they did not experience a sense of separateness from others. The family or the offender may have given the message that this enmeshment was a 'special closeness.' One survivor in the incest healing study (Draucker, 1992) stated:

> I began to realize that my relationship with my father specifically wasn't what I wanted it to be or had always pictured it to be. There was a nurturing part of what we shared together and a real closeness. And I started hearing things about daddy's little girl – red flag. Emotional enmeshment – red flag. You know, things that started sending up all these little signals in me, like, hum, some of what I always felt was real special about our relationship may have actually been rather sick.

Establishing a way to separate self from others becomes an important issue. The same participant described this process for herself in adulthood.

> You see, boundary issues in general, are something that any incest survivor needs to deal with. Since my boundaries in almost every way were totally violated most of my childhood, you know, even emotionally. How far do I let people go with me . . .?

In order to address such issues, counselors may (1) ask for a description of situations in which the survivor experiences boundary dilemmas; (2) assist the survivor in relating these current situations to the abuse experience; and (3) support the survivor's attempts at establishing his or her personal boundaries. In response to the above statement, for example, a counselor might respond with the following inquiries:

> 'Tell me about a situation you experienced recently in which your boundaries were threatened.'
> 'How was that situation similar to (different from) your abuse experience?'
> 'What did you do in the situation?'
> 'In what ways would you have liked to have set limits on the other person's behavior?'
> 'What would it be like for you to set those limits?'

Another participant in the same incest healing study related the following scenario:

> I went to him [a physician] last year and he was new, he was somebody new that I was just going to. And he pulled his stool very close to me and I felt myself extremely uncomfortable. I mean, I was sweating, I could feel my heart racing and I thought 'tell him to get away.' I kind

of kept establishing in my mind what I had a right to establish with
people – that physical boundary. Something kept – I couldn't say it.

In response to a description of a situation such as this, it would be
important for the counselor to support the client's desire to protect
her physical boundaries. A possible counselor response might be:

Your physical space is very important and in this situation the doctor
invaded that space. I support your idea that you have a right to
establish your boundaries. What would you like to have said to the
doctor?

Establishing boundaries may include saying 'no' to unwanted
sexual or physical contact, or to other intrusive or exploitative
behaviors; establishing independent interests and becoming
involved in activities separate from one's significant other; expressing one's opinions or beliefs; expressing one's 'negative' feelings;
and learning to meet one's own needs in a relationship. In some
cases, survivors may choose to end relationships that are dysfunctional, destructive, or abusive. Counseling approaches that
facilitate the above processes can include assertiveness training (or
other interpersonal skills training), group counseling that focuses
on interpersonal dynamics, processing of the relationship between
the counselor and the survivor, parenting skills training, and family
or couples counseling.

Developing trust   For survivors, improving interpersonal relationships also involves learning to trust others. The goal for survivors
is obviously not to indiscriminately trust all, but to be able to make
judgments regarding who in their lives are trustworthy.

This process often begins with the counselor. Sgroi and Bunk
(1988) state that they tell survivors that they do not necessarily
expect the survivors to trust them initially; rather they, as
counselors, will strive to act in a trustworthy manner. For
survivors, learning to trust others is often an issue of accepting that
trust is not an 'all-or-nothing' aspect of a relationship (Hall and
Lloyd, 1989). Rather, it is something that is built gradually and
maintained over time. One cannot evaluate another's trustworthiness by generalizing from one transgression or from one trustworthy act. Counseling can assist survivors in judging the
trustworthiness of others by teaching them to objectively evaluate
the other's behavior in different situations and at different times.

Counseling can also support survivors in reaching out to others,
thereby improving their social support system. One participant in
the incest healing study (Draucker, 1992) described this process for
herself:

My parents have tried to teach me that you don't need anybody, you shouldn't have friends and they don't have good friends. And consequently they're miserable, so they kind of brainwashed me that way. 'You shouldn't need anybody. You can't trust anybody.' Well, I'm not doing that. I like a lot of people and I've made a lot of new friends this semester . . . . I always thought people wouldn't like me so I always stayed away from people. I wouldn't go to parties, wouldn't go out to one of the bars. People liked me but I've always been so afraid no one would like me. And it's not true. I have people tell me, 'I really like you. I'm glad I met you. You're nice. You're fun to be with.' or 'You're really intelligent.' People get really verbally supportive of me and I really need that.

For many survivors, reaching out to others involves developing and practicing new communication and interpersonal skills. These skills may include appropriate self-disclosure (i.e. letting others know of one's personal self), the ability to express affection and caring to others, and the ability to receive affection and caring from others (Sgroi, 1989a). Learning to create personal boundaries and to develop intimate relationships can have a profound effect on survivors' relationships with partners and children. Family therapy can be useful to facilitate these changes.

Sexual functioning

Once survivors have addressed issues of self-esteem and interpersonal relationships, the next step in the healing process is often to address the issue of sexuality. The goal of many survivors at some point in the healing process is to develop a healthy sexual life. The sexuality of survivors is often adversely affected by the childhood sexual abuse experience during which they could not assert their interests, give their consent, control their involvement, or understand what was occurring.

Female survivors and sexuality Maltz and Holman (1987) suggested that basic social and cultural influences (e.g. society's discomfort related to sexuality, poor sex education, misperceptions regarding female sexuality) can often result in guilt, confusion, fear, isolation, and dependency in non-abused adolescent females. Due to the circumstances involved in the experience of childhood sexual abuse, abused adolescent females experience powerlessness and hopelessness in addition. Females develop numerous misconceptions about sexuality and sex roles due to sexual socialization in our culture, and these are further exacerbated by the abuse experience. These misconceptions include beliefs that sexual relations should primarily meet the male's needs and desires; that the role of the female in sexual activity is to be submissive and dependent; that women are the property of men; that women must satisfy the male's sexual desires, which are powerful and uncontrollable; and that, for women, sexual activity is a prerequisite for receiving emotional nurturance from men.

Three aspects of sexuality seem to be influenced by the experience of childhood sexual abuse (Maltz and Holman, 1987). The first aspect is the pattern of sexual emergence in adolescents or young adults. For survivors this often involves either sexual withdrawal (e.g. avoidance of dates) due to sexual fears and low self-esteem, or promiscuous or self-destructive sexual activity due to survivors' needs for attention or proof that they are now in control of their sexuality. The second aspect of sexuality influenced by the sexual abuse experience is the choice of a same-sex or opposite-sex partner. Although the relationship between early childhood sexual abuse and sexual preference is unclear, a sexually victimizing experience can undoubtedly influence the choice of one's sex partners. For example, heterosexual female survivors may choose women as sexual partners because they could be more supportive of the survivors' healing process (e.g. offer more nurturance, be more expressive of feelings, be 'safer') whereas homosexual female survivors may choose a male partner if their victimization experience interfered with their awareness of their sexual preference (Maltz and Holman, 1987). Finally, a childhood experience of abuse often leads to disruptions in sexual functioning manifested in disorders of sexual arousal, response, and satisfaction. Many survivors report that sexual arousal or sexual responses are associated with feelings experienced during the abuse (e.g. disgust, panic) or with trauma symptomatology (e.g. flashbacks).

Male survivors and sexuality   The sexual responses of males to victimization, while resembling the responses of female survivors in many ways, are differentially influenced both by male sex role socialization and by the frequency with which the abuse of males is by another male. For example, male survivors may be more likely to minimize their abuse experience because of society's messages that males are not victims. Also, men are socialized to act on their feelings rather than to express them verbally, so hyper-sexuality, compulsive sexual behaviours, and aggressive sexual behaviors are often exhibited by male survivors. Same-sex behaviors and sexual identity concerns are frequently reported.

Counseling approaches to sexuality issues   Counseling related to sexuality can have an insight-oriented focus, a cognitive focus, and a behavioral focus. Involving sexual partners can be especially beneficial.

Initially, survivors need to make the connection between current sexual difficulties and their abuse experience, in much the same way as they do with other current difficulties. Exploration of how their abuse experiences influenced their sexual development, their choice of sex partners, their sexual self-esteem, and their current sexual functioning is important.

The misconceptions of survivors regarding sex roles and sexuality can be addressed through the use of cognitive challenging or restructuring. Maltz and Holman (1987) discussed the 'Bill of Sexual Rights,' which, when presented to survivors, is helpful in challenging their sexual misconceptions. This 'Bill' includes basic premises such as 'I have a right to my own body,' 'I have a right to set my own sexual limits,' and 'I have a right to experience sexual pleasure' (1987: 83). Cognitive challenges for male survivors might focus on male sexual socialization issues (e.g. 'Men do not cry,' 'Men can protect themselves').

Maltz and Holman (1987) have discussed several behavioral changes survivors can make to deal with sexual problems. These include avoidance of triggers of the abuse experience (e.g. the smell of alcohol, cigarette smoke) during sex, finding a place for sex that is not similar to where the sexual abuse occurred, or learning to say no or to stop sexual activities with one's partner in a non-rejecting manner.

Behaviorally oriented sex therapy with a counselor to treat specific sexual dysfunctions is often indicated. Counselors should generally acquire specific training to employ some of these procedures. Sex therapy techniques may include Masters and Johnson's (1970) squeeze technique for premature ejaculation (i.e. the head of the penis is squeezed by the partner to reduce erection), sensate focusing (i.e. the pairing of pleasurable sensations with relaxation) and graded sexual contact (i.e. engaging in sexual activities from the least to the most threatening) for orgasmic dysfunction and impotence, and desensitization (e.g. relaxation, hypnosis, self-vaginal dilation) for vaginismus.

If the survivor has a committed sexual partner, counseling related to issues of sexuality is often most successful when the partner is included in counseling at some point. Partners may experience feelings of rejection, powerlessness, intense anger toward the survivor's family, or inadequacy for not being able to make the survivor 'better.' The goals of couples' treatment therefore may include helping partners understand and appreciate the impact of the incest on the survivor's life; encouraging the couple to consider that the sexual dysfunction relates to the abuse, not to either partner's inadequacy; and assisting the survivors in responding to their partners' needs and concerns (Maltz and Holman, 1987). Often, couples need to learn to communicate openly with each other regarding their sexual issues. Involvement in sex therapy, using some of the techniques discussed above, often requires that both partners participate actively in treatment.

Case vignette   The following case vignette illustrates how counseling techniques may be combined to address a sexual dysfunction experienced by a female incest survivor. Grace was a 30-year-old woman who sought counseling for vaginismus. She had been sexually abused by her father for several years when she was a young child. Grace originally did not connect her sexual dysfunction with her sexual abuse experience, so this issue was addressed at the start of counseling.

> *Grace:* That [the abuse] happened so long ago. My problem now couldn't be related, could it?
>
> *Counselor:* Often, one's sexual life can continue to be affected by an abuse experience. As a child who was sexually abused you could not control or understand what was happening to you. Your body was violated and you were engaged in sexual activity you did not choose and were not ready for.
>
> *Grace:* Yes, maybe the tightening results from my not wanting to be violated again. But my boyfriend is kind, gentle.
>
> *Counselor:* Yes, although as an adult you've chosen a caring partner, the act of sex can trigger old memories and feelings.
>
> *Grace:* Yes, sometimes after we try to have sex I do have nightmares. I have never truly enjoyed sex. Now that I have a nice boyfriend I think I feel guilty. My father told me no one would love me for me. He called me a whore. Jack loves me, I know. But maybe I still feel dirty, after all these years.

Once Grace understood her sexual dysfunction in the larger context of her abuse experiences, more specific counseling interventions were used. These included:

- Cognitive challenges to Grace's belief that she was a 'whore' who did not deserve to have a good relationship or enjoyable sex. The belief that she had a right to sexual pleasure was extremely difficult for her to accept. She joined a women's sexuality group where this belief was reinforced by other group members.
- The use of relaxation techniques (e.g. warm baths, imagery) and self-vaginal dilation were used to treat the vaginismus. This symptom subsided after three months.

Survivors as offenders In dealing with sexuality issues with survivors, the issue of sexual offending must be addressed. This issue may differ for female and male offenders. Lepine has discussed her counseling experiences with female survivors who have also engaged in sexual offending behaviors. These women continued to experience overwhelming guilt even after working through survivor issues, and would often not disclose their offense to the counselor for some time. Although the percentage of adult female survivors who subsequently sexually abuse others is believed to be very small, the author warned that counselor denial of this possibility can interfere with the recovery of these survivors. Counselors should not dismiss or minimize survivors' guilt related to the offending behavior, nor should they 'join with, support, or exacerbate a disproportionate and disabling sense of guilt' (Lepine, 1990: 274).

Disclosure of offending behavior is facilitated if the survivors have established a trusting relationship with the counselor and if the counselor introduces the issue. Lepine recommended an intervention such as: ' "You know, when women have been sexually abused as children, they sometimes act out sexually against others, too." ' (1990: 275). The counselor should respond calmly to a survivor's disclosure of offending behavior and should non-judgmentally convey the message that, while the behavior is unacceptable, the counselor will not reject the client and will assist her in dealing with this issue. In certain instances (e.g. ongoing abuse), this might involve reporting the offense.

The goal for survivors who have offended is to accept responsibility for their behaviors while ceasing self-destructive behaviors in the service of alleviating their guilt (Lepine, 1990). Counselors may first assist survivors to acknowledge their feelings, including their sexual feelings, and to differentiate between experiencing and expressing feelings. Survivors can then begin to accept responsibility for their sexuality, thereby gaining a sense of control over their sexual behaviors.

Counseling must also address survivors' feelings of guilt stemming from having abused another person. Lepine (1990) recommended the use of the empty-chair technique in which survivors speak vicariously with their victims. Survivors may acknowledge the offense and its consequences, apologize and ask for forgiveness, and share their own abuse experience. Survivors may also communicate these messages to their victims through the use of the unsent letter. Actual contact with a victim, however, should be thoughtfully considered before being carried out by exploring the survivors' motives (e.g. survivors should not expect the victim to resolve their guilt); the consequences (e.g. legal actions, the survivors' reputation); the victim's possible reactions (e.g. trauma symptomatology if the experience had been repressed); and the survivors' own possible reaction to this experience.

Although the goal of counseling an offender is never to minimize the offending behavior, it is helpful for survivors, if they were children or adolescents at the time of the offense, to consider the offense in the context of their developmental stage and in the context of their abuse history. They should not judge their behavior assuming that they had adult resources at the time or that they were unencumbered by their own personal experience of victimization.

The counseling of male survivors who have engaged in sexually offending behavior has also been addressed. In many cases, the typical disclosure process differs from that of female survivors. Female survivors often begin counseling to deal with their abuse, and later in the process reveal the offending behavior. Male survivors, on the other hand, often enter counseling prompted by a sexual offense and reveal their own victimization experience later in the process. These differences may reflect the fact that because women are socialized to care for and protect others, the offending behavior is less frequent, less traumatic, and more likely to cease when they are adults (Lepine, 1990). Males, who are socialized to act out their feelings and to deny their experience of victimization, may be more likely to offend into adulthood in ways that will result in some contact with the criminal justice system, leading ultimately to counseling.

The percentage of male victims who become offenders is unclear. However, the assumption that most male survivors engage in sexually offending behaviors is a destructive myth that can interfere with the healing of survivors. Gerber suggested that, 'It seems more reasonable to acknowledge that according to research, it [transition from victim to offender] occurs with some frequency and causation is attributable to a variety of variables' (1990: 154). These variables include a victimization history of bizarre sexual acts, sexual acts accompanied by threat of violence, the use of a 'seductive, covert, presexual conditioning process' (1990: 155) by the offender, and a long duration. Certain personality characteristics (e.g. passive dependency) and the chemical dependency of the survivor are also contributing factors to the transition from victim to offender.

The counseling of male survivors who are also perpetrators thus involves addressing both the offending behavior and the survivors' own experiences of victimization. Carlson (1990) recommends that counseling begin with perpetrator issues until the client is ready to address his own childhood experiences. Counseling offenders may occur in four stages, which are described by Carlson (1990). The first stage is the focus on perpetrator characteristics, attitudes, and self-concept. Counseling interventions include setting limits; providing structure; and confronting the perpetrator's denial, his view of himself as a victim of the system or of his family, and his tendency to project negative characteristics onto others (e.g. calling his abused daughter a 'slut'). The next stage in counseling is the reinforcement of the client's positive characteristics and the development of his strengths. Counseling interventions include assisting the survivor to develop extra-familial support systems, to strengthen his own boundaries (e.g. develop assertiveness skills), and to learn to delay gratification. Counselors should reinforce other positive behaviors such as the survivor accepting responsibility for his actions, expressing his feelings, and communicating his needs in a direct manner. The next stage, treating the 'victim within,' occurs when the offending behaviors that have served to help the client deal with the abuse begin to subside and issues related to his own victimization begin to emerge. During this stage the counselor provides support, education, and validation related to the client's victimization experiences. The client is encouraged to describe these experiences fully. He can then appreciate that his own victimization was a source of his victimizing behavior, although this does not relieve him of the responsibility for his offenses (Carlson, 1990). When the survivor gets in touch with his own feelings of victimization, he can begin to develop empathy for his victims. The final stage of counseling is called returning the parental role to the client, as the client again assumes responsibility for his own behavior. The client begins to set his own boundaries (e.g. respecting others' privacy, determining appropriate limits with his children) and to determine for himself what constitute appropriate sexual behaviors. He also identifies available sources of support following treatment, methods by which he will care for himself, and a plan of action if he feels he is in danger of re-offending.

Case example

The case of Jerry, which was discussed in the preceding chapter, also exemplifies the process of making desired life changes once the connections between childhood experiences and adult functioning are made. Jerry made changes in his self-concept, in his relationships with his wife and family of origin, and ultimately in his job.

Much of counseling focused on Jerry's self-esteem. Jerry originally described himself as an 'insignificant failure.' Also, he believed himself to be 'unmanly,' a self-perception that was probably related to his abuse experience involving same-sex offenders. The following client–counselor interaction shows how self-esteem issues were addressed with Jerry, based on Peplau's model (O'Toole and Welt, 1989).

Jerry: I guess I'm not much of anything. I'm certainly not much of a man. ['Self-view in awareness']

Counselor: Where did you get the message that you are not much of anything?

Jerry: I guess from my family. My dad never bothered with me much, except to yell when he was drunk, or to tell me what to do at work. My mom, well, she thought it best we kids be 'seen and not heard.' She was pretty weak. I wanted more to do with her but she was always sick.

Counselor: So both of your parents gave you the message, in one way or another, that you were not very important. Tell me about an experience you had when you felt particularly unimportant.

Jerry: Once, I brought home a table I made in shop, you know, woodworking class. I thought it was good. I put it in the living room. I thought my mom would be happy but instead she had me put it out in the garage so my dad 'wouldn't be upset with such clutter.' I was upset because the instructor had said the table was really good.

Counselor: I can see why a young boy would not feel very important in this situation. Something you made yourself, which had received praise, was discarded in the interest of keeping your dad calm.

Jerry: Yes, and shop was the only thing I was really good in. ['Maybe me self-view']

Counselor: You had a talent that was not recognized by your parents but was recognized by your teacher. Were there other situations like this – instances when your parents did not attend to you, but others did?

Jerry: Jean, of course, She was good to me, until she left home. No one else until Jane . . . .

Counselor: Although your parents gave you the message you weren't very important, Jean, and later Jane, showed that you were important to them.

Jerry could describe receiving messages from his parents indicating that he was not considered a significant member of the family and that it was best if he just stayed out of the way. Once Jerry recognized that his self-perceptions stemmed from these messages rather than from his own inherent worthlessness, he did consider other ways of viewing himself. He concluded that he was special to Jean, and that she did support him, as much as she was able, when they were children. He was thus worthwhile in someone's eyes. Jerry also gradually began to consider his strengths: that he had survived his childhood, had maintained a basically sound marriage, and had developed many skills related to his trade. Some of these views were associated with anxiety as they were not how Jerry was accustomed to perceiving himself. For example, Jerry was initially very resistant to considering himself a skillful tradesperson as this meant he might be valued outside the family shop and therefore vocational opportunities might exist for him away from his family.

Eventually, Jerry was seen in counseling with his wife, Jane. He had never told her of the abuse and chose to do so during a counseling session. She was extremely supportive, although some tension developed between Jane and Jerry as she expressed much anger toward his family whom she 'never liked anyway.' She had trouble understanding why Jerry would have any loyalty remaining toward his family. Nonetheless, she was able to assure Jerry that she did not blame him for the infertility, nor did she see him as 'unmanly.' She did, however, need him to understand her feelings of loss. Once Jerry stopped blaming himself for the infertility, he was able to be more available to her. However, Jerry felt unable to 'talk about his feelings,' as this was basically prohibited in his family of origin. Thus, the development of new communication skills became the focus of counseling for this couple. Both Jerry and Jane became more successful in expressing their needs and feelings in ways the other could hear. The couple did not require behaviorally-oriented sex therapy, because their sexual relationship improved as their communication skills developed.

Jerry chose not to confront his parents or Tom about the abuse but did identify the need to separate from his family. He made the difficult decision to leave the machine shop, and began work at a different plant. He interacted with his family only occasionally, when he chose to do so. He did well in his new position, ultimately being appointed as shift supervisor.

7

Addressing Resolution Issues

Once survivors have begun to successfully employ new coping mechanisms and make desired life changes, they often deal with issues related to resolution of the childhood sexual abuse experience. Resolution does not indicate that the experience of abuse is forgotten, or that the healing process is finished. Indeed, many survivors believe that that healing can be a lifelong process (Draucker, 1992). Resolution here refers to the process by which the childhood sexual abuse experience is integrated into the individual's identity, but is no longer the primary force that guides his or her adult life. Sgroi (1989a) refers to this process as relinquishing the survivor identity. The individual views him or herself from a multidimensional perspective and assumes total responsibility for their own destiny. The issues discussed below seem to be frequently related to the process of resolution.

Forgiveness

Many survivors, after they have experienced some healing from the sexual abuse experience, begin to struggle with the issue of whether or not to forgive the offender. Some survivors believe that this is a prerequisite to being 'truly recovered,' and some believe that they must forgive the offender because of their religious or social beliefs. It can be important for counselors to help survivors determine the meaning forgiveness has for them. Maltz and Holman (1987) discussed two 'styles' of forgiveness. In the first 'style,' survivors release the offender from responsibility for the abuse because they have determined that the offender's actions were justifiable in some way. This concept of forgiveness may represent survivors' attempts to close the healing process prematurely by denying repressed anger, hurt, or betrayal toward the offender and may be a form of self-blame or minimization. The second 'style' of forgiveness involves coming to appreciate the offender's 'humanness, limitations, and history' (1987: 31). This process typically includes achieving an understanding of the offender's own childhood abuse experiences or his or her adult weaknesses or pathology. The authors believe that this 'style' of forgiveness can be beneficial for survivors as it can facilitate their development of compassion and forgiveness for themselves.

Hall and Lloyd (1989) suggest that forgiveness occurs when survivors accept their feelings related to the abuse, especially their anger, but they no longer seek revenge against the offender. This type of forgiveness can be beneficial for survivors, as it further frees them from ties to the offender. If survivors no longer need to avenge the offense, the offender becomes less relevant in their healing process and survivors come closer to accepting responsibility for their adult happiness.

The survivors' religious or philosophical beliefs related to forgiveness must be discussed, acknowledged, and respected. However, forgiveness that stems from survivors' true acceptance of their feelings, from insight into the offender's childhood experiences and adult limitations, and from personal healing that has moved the survivors beyond the need for revenge is usually more meaningful for the survivor than forgiveness that is dictated by religious or social prescriptions.

Counseling can focus on helping survivors determine the personal meaning they attach to forgiveness and on helping them determine the role forgiveness might play in their own healing process. Survivors may choose, for example, to forgive a non-offending parent, but not the offender. In order to resolve this issue for themselves, they must realize that forgiveness is not a prerequisite to their healing, but is a personal choice some survivors may make as they begin to move toward a resolution of their abuse experience.

The following client–counselor interaction illustrates a survivor's struggle with the issue of forgiveness. Pamela is a 23-year-old woman who was sexually abused as a child by her older brother.

Pamela: My visit [to her family] did not go well this weekend. I was talking to my mother and she said she believes to be 'truly healed' I must forgive my brother. She's brought this up before.

Counselor: What is it like for you when your mom says this?

Pamela: I get really angry. I think she wants this whole thing to be over and done with so he [Pamela's brother] can come back into our lives and we can pretend it [the abuse] never happened. I don't know, though, maybe at some point I will be able to forgive him. Not now, but at some point maybe. I don't know.

Counselor: You were angry then at your mom because you sense her push for you to forgive your brother comes more from her needs to reunite the family than from her concern about your healing?

Pamela: Yes, all along she has been more concerned about getting things back to normal. I'm not saying I'll never forgive him. I'm just not ready yet. And I don't want to be pushed. But someday I hope I will reach a point of forgiveness.

Counselor: Sometimes people mean different things when they talk about forgiveness. When you say at some point you may be able to forgive your brother, what do you mean?

Pamela: Well, not that I'll say that the abuse was 'OK.' I'll never say that. It wasn't. It hurt me deeply and that will never change. Maybe at some point though I won't feel as much hatred. At one point I wanted him dead. I know he did to me what was done to him. Yet, that doesn't make it OK. I don't know. I'm confused.

Counselor: Yes, one meaning of forgiveness is that one 'forgives and forgets' the abuse, coming to believe it was unimportant and should be forgotten. Perhaps you believe this is what your mom wants you to do. Another meaning of forgiveness is that one reaches some understanding of why the abuse occurred and then moves beyond needing retribution. One can still feel angry but is no longer driven by bitterness.

Pamela: Yes, it was somehow helpful to know Grandpa abused Tim [her brother]. Although that didn't make what he did to me OK, it somehow helped make things make sense, if you know what I mean. I would like to be able to be in the same room with him without freaking. Maybe then I'll feel more like he can't 'pull my strings' any longer.

Reintegrating into the family of origin

Many survivors find it necessary to discontinue or to limit contact with their family of origin when they begin the healing process. In some cases, survivors need distance from the dysfunctional nature of their family in order to appreciate the impact the dynamics of their family had on their development. Some survivors break off contact because family members continue to engage in behaviors related to the abuse experience that are deleterious to the survivor's recovery (e.g. blaming the survivor for the abuse, sabotage of the survivor's healing). For example, one survivor in the incest healing study (Draucker, 1992) reported that, 'I didn't talk to my family for two years. I withdrew from them after a really severe confrontation about counseling, which they really objected to.'

However, many survivors, after they have experienced some healing, decide to re-establish contact with their family of origin. The same survivor stated:

> And as soon as my counseling sessions had ended, I found out my mom had cancer, so it was like, you were able to spend two years away in healing and getting over it, then it was like time to go back and slay the dragons and see my brothers and sisters and talk to my mom and try and work through some of the problems and feelings that I had with them, which I thought I did pretty well.

Whether survivors are re-establishing contact with their family after a separation or are continuing ongoing contact with their family, they need to approach family contact based on the changes they have made in the healing process, rather than interacting with their family based on old roles and patterns. Participants in the incest healing study (Draucker, 1992), for example, stressed that the re-establishment of contact with their family had to be, in some way, on the survivors' terms, which were often specific and definite. One survivor maintained a relationship with her brother, the offender, as long as he remained in therapy. Another agreed to see her parents, with whom she had broken off contact, if they came to therapy with her to address their role in the family dysfunction. One survivor, who had been abused by her stepfather, discussed re-establishing a relationship with her mother, which she planned to discontinue again if her mother engaged in any 'hurtful or destructive' behaviors (e.g. blaming the survivor for the abuse) from which she had agreed to refrain.

Reintegrating into the family of origin, based on changes survivors have made, can be an important resolution issue. Although the survivors' desire to resume or maintain contact with their family of origin should be validated by the counselor, it is helpful to determine if the survivors have any unrealistic expectations (e.g. that the family will have changed in a way to meet the survivors' needs). Most typically, families will attempt to repeat old, familar patterns to maintain the status quo. It could be harmful if survivors allow the actions of their family once again to control their sense of well-being. Counseling may be helpful in assisting survivors to maintain realistic expectations regarding their family's responses while focusing on what survivors can do themselves when re-entering the family or when re-establishing a relationship with a family member.

Davis (1990) has proposed an activity that assists survivors in establishing new ground rules or setting limits when interacting with their families. She asks survivors to determine what things they would no longer do with their family (e.g. care for an inebriated parent) as well as what things they will no longer discuss with their family (e.g. the survivor's sexual life). Davis also encourages survivors to specify the conditions under which they will have contact with their family (e.g. only at the survivor's residence; at the family's home only if the offender is not present). Counselors can use a similar procedure and discuss with survivors issues such as how they can best communicate these ground rules to their family, what the experience of setting limits might be like for them, what their 'contingency' plan will be if the ground rules are not respected, and how they anticipate their family will respond. Family members will usually 'test the limits', and survivors should be prepared for this.

What is most important is that survivors do not engage in old family dynamics in which they are exploited, manipulated, ignored, or belittled. In some instances contact continues to be destructive, and survivors choose to break off their relationship with the family, either permanently or temporarily. This decision is often accompanied by sadness and grief, and these feelings must be validated by the counselor. This 'letting go' of the family of origin, or the coming to terms with their limitations, can be a significant part of the resolution process.

Finding meaning in the experience

Taylor has maintained that one way to cope with a traumatic or a victimizing experience is by searching for meaning in the experience. She defined meaning as 'an effort to understand the event: why it happened and what impact it has had' (1983: 1161). Finding meaning includes determining the cause of the event and the significance of the event on one's life. Research (Draucker, 1989; Silver et al., 1983) has suggested that this process is important for incest survivors and may facilitate the resolution of the abuse experience.

Understanding the cause of the event is a process referred to as casual attribution. This process has been discussed so far primarily in relation to survivors' reattributing the cause of the abuse from themselves to the offender. Although holding the offender responsible for the abuse is important in addressing issues of self-blame, for many survivors simply determining that the abuse was the offender's fault does not seem to be a sufficient explanation. Many question why the offender did what he or she did, why the abuse occurred in their family, and, ultimately, why society permits the widespread occurrence of childhood sexual abuse.

In a study of incest survivors (Draucker, in press), several participants indicated that they had answered these questions for themselves. Several reported that they had learned that their offenders were impaired in some way (e.g. alcoholic, psychotic). One participant stated: 'My father was an alcoholic who was raised in a time when women were inferior. He was also sick.' Other survivors attributed the actions of the offenders to the offenders' own history of abuse. One stated: '[It was my] older brother taking out aggressions on me, most likely caused by his own molestation from our paternal grandmother.' Several survivors attributed the cause of the abuse to the dynamics in their families. For example, a participant stated: 'I realize that the incest experience was because of my dysfunctional family, not because of me.' One survivor placed the blame for the incest on society. She stated that she had come to believe that the incest was part of 'an extreme exploitation of females commonly practiced in the USA.'

Whether certain types of attribution are more helpful in facilitating healing is uncertain. What is important in regard to resolution is that survivors meet their need to come up with a satisfactory causal explanation, rather than accepting that their abuse was a chance occurrence. This need was described by Chodoff et al. (1964) when discussing how parents of children with malignant diseases cope with their experience: 'To combat such an intolerable possibility (chance), the parents sought for an acceptable answer to the question, "why did it happen," exhibiting as they did some particular aspect of a universal, even an existential hunger for a meaningful and understandable explanation of seemingly indifferent events' (1964: 747).

Counselors may facilitate survivors' exploration of the question 'why.' The goal of this process is not to exonerate the offender from the responsibility for the abuse, or even to precipitate forgiveness; rather, it is to provide an explanation that allows survivors to place their abuse in a meaningful context. In some cases it is helpful for the counselor to provide factual or 'theoretical' material to aid in this exploration. For example, discussing incestuous family dynamics as outlined by Gelinas (1983) may help survivors understand the functioning of their family, and discussing incest from a feminist perspective (e.g. according to Herman, 1981) may help survivors put their childhood sexual abuse in a larger societal context. Reading literature can also facilitate this process. Daugherty (1984), for example, wrote a book for survivors of childhood sexual abuse entitled *Why me?* In one chapter the author addresses the issue of understanding individuals who sexually abuse children. Seemingly, this seeks to help survivors with their need to know 'why' the abuser did what he or she did.

Taylor (1983) also indicated that finding meaning involves coming to understand the significance the traumatic event has had on one's life. She suggested that this could involve construing positive meaning from the experience by reappraising one's life, developing a new attitude toward life, or gaining increased self-knowledge. Incest survivors have described engaging in these processes as part of healing (Draucker, in press). They indicated that because of the abuse they are stronger, more self-reliant, or independent; have a greater self-awareness of their emotional or spiritual life; have acquired a sense of purpose in life; or have developed a better understanding of human nature in general. Wiehe, who made a survey of 150 victims of sibling abuse, also reported that some of the respondents saw a 'silver lining in the dark cloud of their abuse' (1990: 132) and identified using their abuse experience for personal growth.

It may be that part of resolving the abuse experience, for some survivors, involves the 'rethinking of one's attitude or priorities to restructure one's life along more satisfying lines' (Taylor, 1983: 1163) and attributing these changes to the abuse experience. This does not mean that survivors conclude that they were glad the abuse occurred or that the offender actually 'did them a favor' and is therefore exonerated. Rather, they conclude that the abuse was a negative event, but from that event, or from the healing process of that event, they were able to grow personally in some way.

Counselors can help survivors to discuss the process of finding meaning by inquiring about survivors' beliefs related to 'why' abuse occurs and by exploring survivors' perceptions of the significance the experience has ultimately had on them. One survivor (Draucker, in press) stated: 'It [the abuse] has forced my growth in areas that would have been neglected otherwise. I have to examine how much of our behavior is choice versus reactions – where's the balance?'

In the following client–counselor interaction, a survivor struggles with the issue of finding meaning in her incest experience. Rosalie is a 55-year-old woman who was sadistically sexually abused as a child by her uncle.

Rosalie: You know, I realized that as much suffering as I have experienced – it's been almost fifty years of suffering – I don't think I would be as strong as I am today if it hadn't been for what he did.
Counselor: In what ways are you stronger than you would have been?
Rosalie: After being in therapy, I now know that I can handle just about anything. If I lived through what I did as a youngster, I can live through anything. I never realized that before. My friend Eleanor falls apart at every family crisis. In fact, the other day someone called me a 'tough cookie.' I think that's true. I am a 'tough cookie.' I wouldn't wish what happened to me on a dog, but it did make me strong.
Counselor: So having survived a horrible experience as a child . . . .
Rosalie: Yes, I survived because I was strong. I feel good about myself now. I like who I am. Someone asked me if I'm glad the abuse happened. That's nonsense. Of course I'm not glad. I work to stop abuse. But it was one of the many things that made me who I am today. And I like me.

The process of helping others

The need to help others who have been abused, or the need to make the world a safer place more generally, seems to be an important part of the resolution process for many survivors. In the incest healing study (Draucker, 1992), for example, the majority of participants identified that having a positive impact on their world – by helping other victims personally, by being an advocate for victims, or by choosing a helping vocation (e.g. teaching) – was an important aspect of their own recovery. In a study that investigated the process of construing benefit from a negative experience of incest (Draucker, in press), the majority of survivors who found any benefit in the experience listed the ability to help others as a positive outcome. These survivors indicated that, as a result of their incest experience, they were able to help others in a way that non-abused individuals could not, because they had acquired a special ability to empathize with those who were suffering, the courage to speak out against injustice, a unique skill to detect abuse in their work settings (e.g. a pediatric emergency room), and an increased ability to protect their own children from abuse.

Helping others may be one way survivors make sense of their incest experiences. Some counselors have addressed this need in group treatment programs. Gordy (1983), for example, described an activity in which the survivors listed, from their own experiences, the signs and symptoms of childhood sexual abuse in a family in order to alert professionals to the possibility of abuse in the lives of children with whom they work.

Helping activities seem to be beneficial for survivors when they have worked through a number of issues in their own healing process (e.g. caretaking issues, setting boundaries with others, dealing with shame). For example, it can be a devastating experience for survivors to speak publicly about their abuse when they have not worked through their feelings of shame. Also, if survivors choose to actively help other survivors before they have learned to define their own boundaries or to set interpersonal limits, they may end up feeling burdened or overwhelmed. The counselor may help survivors explore the role that helping others can play in the healing process and support these activities when they contribute to the resolution of the survivors' abuse experience.

Addressing identity issues

The key resolution issue for incest survivors is establishing a clear sense of their own identity. Much of the healing process has focused on survivors' giving up the role of victim by taking control of their thoughts, feelings, and actions. When survivors perceive that they have given up this role they often mourn this loss, as the victim role probably has defined their identity for some time. Along with the role of the victim, survivors also often give up their dysfunctional caretaking roles, which may have shaped their interpersonal relationships and perhaps even their vocational choices. Feelings of loss and anxiety need to be validated and survivors often need to discuss what they are losing (e.g. counseling, caretaking and concern from others, a support system of other survivors) when they give up old roles and behaviors.

Sgroi maintained that ultimately survivors can give up the survivor identity as well. This occurs when they have completed all the tasks of recovery and view themselves from a 'multidimensional perspective' (1989a: 128). Survivors recognize their strengths and weaknesses and have integrated the sexual abuse experience into their total identity. They have found success in adopting new coping mechanisms and have assumed responsibility for their own happiness, so they no longer need to define themselves in terms of their experience of childhood sexual abuse. Sgroi (1989a) suggested that this stage can be 'elusive' for survivors. Counselors, in the later stages of treatment, might well discuss with the client the process of giving up the survivor identity. One participant in the incest healing study (Draucker, 1992) discussed this process for herself:

> Another thing I think I dealt with was to try to get rid of the role of incest survivor. I used to play with it by saying, no, I was a survivor. Because of it, a lot of good things were given to me. I understand, I could empathize, I could do a lot of things that way and that I was a survivor. I was getting on with my life and all that. . . . Dr Susan Forward was in this area and a lot of women were calling [to a radio program] and she would talk to them and she had been an incest victim herself and had written a book which I had read and her idea was to get out of the role of being an incest survivor and do your life without having to be in that role. I liked that idea. I worked very hard on trying to just not constantly come from, dwell on, be, an incest survivor.

Termination of counseling

Along with resolution comes the process of termination of counseling. This, of course, can represent a significant loss for the survivor, but also a transition consistent with relinquishing the survivor identity. A review of the healing process, reminiscence of the highlights of counseling, a sharing of feelings between counselor and client regarding the relationship, an exploration of the client's future plans, and a discussion of the client and the counselor's feelings related to termination are all part of the termination process. Many counselors choose to extend an invitation to survivors to 'keep in touch', as survivors often profit from sharing ongoing life changes with the counselor. However, the counselor should help the client differentiate termination related to resolution from the temporary hiatuses in counseling that are due to planned therapeutic, but temporary, counseling breaks and breaks prompted by other factors (e.g. moves, financial difficulties, other life events). This differentiation can reinforce the resolution process by providing closure for the counseling experience.

Case example

The following case is described to exemplify how one of the issues discussed above, reintegrating into the family of origin, can be related to resolution for survivors. Candy was a 22-year-old college student who had attended counseling for approximately one year to deal with having been sexually abused by her brother, Ken. The abuse occurred intermittently for approximately a year when she was 7 and he was 15. The sexual activities primarily included genital fondling, although Candy believed vaginal penetration was attempted on some occasions. Ken had been adopted at the age of 2, at a time when Candy's parents believed they could not have any biological children. Ken exhibited significant behavioral problems (e.g. being expelled from school, minor scrapes with the law, unruliness at home) throughout most of his childhood. He was ultimately diagnosed as having fetal alcohol syndrome. As an adult, he continued to live with his parents, worked at a local service station, and spent most of this time with his local 'buddies.'

After being in counseling for over six months, Candy had decided to tell her parents about the abuse during one of her visits home. She reported to her counselor that her father responded only by saying, 'I should kill him next time I see him.' Candy's mother initially became 'hysterical' and was unable to discuss Candy's experience with her. However, on their next contact, Candy's mother began to defend Ken and minimize the abuse. She suggested to Candy that the abuse was 'normal child's play,' that Ken probably did not mean any harm, and that perhaps the counselor was making 'too big a deal' of the issue. Candy's father would not discuss the abuse further.

Although Candy had spent time in counseling preparing for this disclosure, she stated that she was nonetheless 'devastated' by her parents' response and decided to limit her weekly visits with them. Initially she would see them occasionally, on major holidays, but this also become stressful and she ceased these visits as well. Candy's mother wrote to her frequently, 'begging' her to come home. Her letters often contained references to her ill-health and despondency over Candy's break from the family.

Her parents' reactions to her disclosure prompted Candy to examine their roles as non-offending parents. Initially, she had assumed that they had no knowledge of the abuse, but she eventually began to wonder if her mother 'knew on some level.' Candy believed that she did not tell her mother about the abuse at the time it occurred because her mother 'pampered' Ken and, as a child, Candy believed her mother would 'fall apart' if she knew what 'her children were doing.' Candy stated that she would never have considered telling her father, who was seldom at home and who would not 'talk about personal things anyway.'

Candy struggled for some time in counseling to understand her parents' role in the abuse situation as well as their reactions to her disclosure of the abuse. This led to a discussion of her parents' family backgrounds. Candy reported that her mother grew up in poverty and was raised by several aunts, at least two of whom were apparently prostitutes. She had spent her later years in a foster home and met her husband, Candy's father, during her last year of high school. Candy knew less of her father's history, other than that he came from a strict, but respectable, military family. Candy's parents tried to have a child for many years, finally adopting Ken through a Catholic adoption agency. Candy herself was a 'late miracle' baby.

Candy stated that her mother always seemed overwhelmed by child-care responsibilities with Ken: 'She was always going to school or to court or to counseling to deal with his problems.' Candy suspected that her mother had become 'overinvolved' with her son, whereas her father withdrew, having as little to do as possible with Ken or with the family. Candy, as a child, was quiet and caused 'no problems.' As an adolescent, she became her mother's confidante. Her mother frequently complained to Candy about the lack of support she received from Candy's dad, a 'workaholic,' and the troubles she continued to have with Ken.

Candy began to piece together that her mother had probably married her father seeking the respectability and stability she lacked as a child. Although her mother's marriage provided those things, Candy surmised that her father provided little nurturance and caring. When Ken began to have problems, her mother took total responsibility for him. Candy guessed that her mother probably felt like a failure because she had been so invested in having the 'All-American' family and was unable to 'make Ken better.' As Ken's problems increased, her father withdrew further, adding to her mother's feelings of burden and abandonment. Her pregnancy with Candy, which at one time would have been welcomed, was unplanned and probably added to her mother's stress. After achieving some understanding of these dynamics, Candy decided to resume contact with her mother. In the following interaction, she and the counselor discuss this issue:

Candy: I have decided to see my mom again. I feel better myself and I miss her. I don't need to see Dad, but I do want to see Mom. I've been away long enough. When I see her though, I'm afraid I'll slip back. That's what kept me from calling her. I've come so far myself. But I also want to talk with her about some of what we've been talking about, you know, her background and stuff.

Counselor: I know you've been wanting to be involved with your mom again. That's important to you. In what ways are you afraid you'll slip back if you see her again?

Candy: Well, it hurt me so much last time when my mom defended Ken and made light of the abuse. Then she got sick. Remember . . . I got real depressed. That could happen again. That's why I hope she's changed.

Counselor: We discussed your mom's response when you told her about the sexual abuse and I know you've determined that her defense of Ken and denial of the abuse probably results from her long-standing need to have a 'normal, perfect' family and that it is her pattern to withdraw from her problems by becoming ill.

Candy: I know, but maybe she's changed and can face it now. Maybe my staying away shook her up enough . . . . Maybe she'll stand up to my brother to show me she really believes he did something wrong. That would help me and she says she wants to help me.

Counselor: Facing the abuse and dealing with your brother in a way that would be helpful for you would be a major change in your mom's way of dealing with things . . . .

Candy: Yes, it is probably highly unlikely, I know.

Counselor: You are hoping for a significant change. Although your mom loves you and may sincerely want to help you, there is a strong pull for family members to stay the same. To change is threatening.

Candy: I so wish she would be different. She probably won't be. I guess I know that on some level.

Counselor: When you resume contact with your family, you cannot make them change in ways you would like them to. No one has that control over others. You may hope for certain changes while also considering what's realistic.

Candy: I'm afraid if I go back, and she hasn't changed, she'll just make light of the whole thing again.

Counselor: Although you cannot control how your mom responds to you, you can control how you respond to her.

Candy: I know what's coming. [*Smiles*] Because she makes light of the whole thing, I don't have to.

Counselor: Yes, you've made many changes. One change is that you no longer blame yourself for what happened. You seem to hold that belief very strongly now. You accept that the abuse was a traumatic event in your life. Your mom cannot take that away.

Candy: No, she cannot. I do believe that. I guess I also know that without some kind of help, like counseling, she won't change. That makes me sad. I wish she would get help, to understand what did happen to me, and to help herself as well. Otherwise, although I'll never blame myself again, if she defends Ken, I will get frustrated with her and probably stay away again. If only she would get help, I think that's the only way we can be really close again.

Counselor: Although you cannot make her go to counseling, you can ask her to do that and decide how you will proceed with your relationship based on her response.

Candy: Yes, she needs counseling before we really get back together.

Candy therefore determined that she was firm in her belief that the abuse was a significant, traumatic experience, and that contact with her mother could no longer jeopardize this belief. However, she concluded that to resume a meaningful relationship with her mother, her mother would need to confront what had happened to Candy and together they would have to address the family's dynamics. Candy agreed to resume contact with her mother at this point only if her mother agreed to attend counseling with her. Although her mother consented to this, she was extremely reluctant, missing several early sessions due to illness and continually crying throughout the sessions she did attend. However, she eventually confirmed much of what Candy had inferred about her mother's background. Candy's mother also revealed that she had 'suspected' the abuse but could not 'face' it. She confessed that she had feared that if her husband found out what Ken was doing, he would have forced Ken leave the home, something he had continually threatened to do anyway as Ken's problems increased. At this point, Candy expressed rage toward her mother because she had chosen to protect Ken rather than Candy. Interestingly, her mother was not only able to tolerate Candy's expression of rage but was able to agree that she had, in fact, sacrificed Candy due to her own limitations and fears (e.g. of her husband, of Ken, of what others would think). This event was significant for Candy as it 'cemented' many of the issues she had addressed earlier in counseling related to her own self-blame. Her mother also acknowledged that she believed that the abuse was a traumatic experience for Candy and she deeply regretted not intervening to stop it.

Candy also eventually agreed to visit the family home, something she had not done since her initial disclosure of the abuse to her parents. In the following client–counselor interaction Candy discusses her concerns about visiting her family in their home and decides on ground rules that she needs to establish.

Candy: My parents want me to come home and I want to go there, I think, I'm not sure. My brother will be there and I'm not ready to see him yet. He's loud and butts into all conversations. He invades my space. Everyone just puts up with it. Also, I'm ready to see my dad, I think, but I feel really uncomfortable because my mother fusses over him so. She waits on him hand and foot. I'll be expected to do that too. You know, bring him coffee, soda, when he can get it himself. My mother does this for my brother sometimes as well. It makes me sick.

Counselor: You are concerned, then, that if you go home things will be the way they were before. And that you will fall into old habits – 'putting up' with your brother's behavior, waiting on your father.

Candy: Yes, but now I couldn't stand doing those things.

Counselor: Yes, because you've made changes. Putting up with your brother's behaviors is a passive thing to do and you've been working on actively setting limits on the intrusive behaviors of others. 'Waiting on' your dad is a deferent behavior, also something you've been working on avoiding.

Candy: I'm so afraid in that house I'll fall back into doing those things.

Counselor: Again, you cannot control what others do but you can decide what you will or will not do and what you will or will not tolerate there.

Candy: OK, then, I decide here and now that I will not wait on my dad or my brother. And I will tell them this upfront.

Counselor: Yes, you cannot decide if your mother will wait on them but you can decide whether you will or not. What will it be like for you to set this limit?

Candy: It was scary when I heard myself saying it. But it feels good. I know I can do it. I can say no. 'Dad, I will not get your coffee when I'm visiting.' Wow. That felt good. If they don't accept that, I'll leave. My brother is a different story, though. I think his very presence will bother me a lot. Especially since I'm not ready to confront him about the abuse.

Counselor: What would you like to do about your brother?

Candy: Really, I don't want to see him at all.

Counselor: How can you have that happen?

Candy: Well, I can visit when he's not there. I can agree to go only when he's out. A ground rule will be that if Ken's there, I won't be. I won't have him there until I'm ready. If Mom wants me home, she'll have to ensure that Ken will not be there.

Candy identified unhealthy family patterns in which she no longer wanted to participate and determined how to avoid such participation by specifying what she would not do (i.e. 'wait on' the men in the family) and by establishing an important ground rule (i.e. she would not visit when her brother was present). On several occasions Candy recognized attempts by family members to test her limits. For example, during one visit her mother was carrying a coffee cup to her dad in the living room and stopped to answer the phone. Without saying a word, she handed the cup to Candy. At that point, Candy realized she could put the cup down or bring it to her father. She chose to put the cup on the counter, reinforcing her choice not to 'wait on' him. On one occasion the family 'forgot' to make arrangements for Ken to be away from the home for Candy's visit. Consistent with her 'contingency plan,' Candy left immediately and visited a high school friend instead of spending the afternoon with her family.

Eventually Candy chose to confront Ken about the abuse. He responded by becoming sullen and withdrawn, but did not deny the abuse had occurred. Candy grew very aware of his limitations and, although she did not address the issue of forgiveness, she claimed that she had gotten in touch with how 'pathetic' her brother had become.

After this confrontation, Candy began to visit her family less frequently, having decided that she needed to work on developing friendships at school. So she was now withdrawing from her family because it was the 'normal thing to do at [my] age.' However, she believed reintegrating into her family in a 'healthy' way (e.g. by no longer 'keeping the secret,' by setting limits based on her own needs) allowed her the freedom to move on and to begin to establish her own adult relationships.

8
Group Counseling

Group counseling for survivors of childhood sexual abuse is an effective treatment modality, especially when used in conjunction with individual counseling. Receiving confrontation and support from those who have shared similar life experiences and having the opportunity to help others can be especially powerful for survivors. The goals of group counseling, the focus of different types of survivor group, the issues to consider in planning a survivors' group, and the issues that often arise as groups progress are addressed.

Goals of group counseling

Although the specific goals of different types of survivors' groups vary, there are several goals that many groups often share. These include:

decreasing feelings of isolation, stigma, and shame;
challenging survivors' perceptions of themselves as different;
increasing feelings of self-esteem;
instilling hope for recovery;
developing trust in others;
developing interpersonal skills;
retrieving repressed memories;
developing a social support network

Types of survivor group

There are basically two types of group for individuals who were sexually abused as children. Survivors may participate in either a support, or self-help, group or in a clinical, or professionally led, group. There are several different formats (e.g. open ended, time limited) used in clinical groups. Counselors, when planning to run a survivors' group or when referring clients to a survivors' group, should consider the pros and cons of the type and the format of the group and determine if a particular group will meet the needs of their clients.

Support groups

Support, or self-help, survivor groups are organized by survivors themselves and operate without a clinically trained leader. These groups seek to avoid power differentials created in groups conducted by individuals who assume a leadership role by virtue of clinical training rather than by virtue of having survived childhood sexual abuse. An example of a self-help group for survivors of childhood sexual abuse is Incest Survivors Anonymous, a 12-step program based on the principles of Alcoholics Anonymous.

Such self-help programs have the advantage of offering survivors comradeship, support, understanding, recognition, and confrontation in groups that are easily accessible and often free of charge (Gil, 1990). In many cases, these groups provide a surrogate extended family (Gil, 1990). Self-help groups can, however, experience turbulence when intra-group conflict or power issues are not managed successfully or when the group is unable to met the safety needs of members with serious psychiatric symptoms (e.g. psychosis, suicidality). Typically, self-help groups do not use screening procedures (Gil, 1990). Continuity may also be a problem for some survivor groups, as these groups may not have expectations for regular attendance and group leadership may frequently change. Nonetheless, survivors who are in counseling may find involvement in self-help groups beneficial at some point in their healing process, especially when they are ready to withdraw from or supplement their counseling experience.

Clinical groups

The second type of survivor group is the professionally-led counseling group that is usually run in a mental health or social service agency. Several different formats can be used for clinical groups. They can be closed, structured, and time-limited (Bruckner and Johnson, 1987; Cole, 1985; Goodman and Nowak-Scibelli, 1985; Gordy, 1983; Herman and Schatzow, 1984; Tsai and Wagner, 1978); open, unstructured, and ongoing (Blake-White and Kline, 1985), or a combination of the two (Sgroi, 1989b). The advantages and disadvantages of each format will be outlined and discussions of groups described in the literature that have been run according to each format will be included as examples.

Short-term, structured groups Short-term, structured groups typically have a limited number of sessions, run according to a predetermined plan, and limit group membership to those who enter the group at the beginning. These groups have also been referred to as programmatic groups (Briere, 1989). There are several advantages to this group format. In closed groups, members all begin at the same time and are able to explore similar issues simultaneously, thereby enhancing group cohesiveness. Group activities and ground rules provide a structure to facilitate group development. Also, some survivors prefer to have a specified ending point as a parameter to the group experience. Shorter groups usually limit conflict between members (Cole, 1985) allowing them to focus specifically on the sexual abuse experience.

This type of group format also has several potential disadvantages. With a shorter time limit, some members may have difficulty feeling safe or developing a commitment to the group. Members may feel as if they have little control over the course of the group as the focus of each session is predetermined. Also, if a closed group was started before a survivor decided to join, he or she would have to wait until a new group began. This can be difficult once the survivor has decided to risk group involvement.

Cole (1985) described an incest survivors' group led by a female therapist at a women's counseling center. This group is discussed here as an example of a short-term, structured, closed group. The group was conducted for six sessions with each session lasting two hours. Each participant attended an intake session during which they were given literature related to sexual abuse to read prior to the start of the group. The goals and activities of each group session are outlined.

Session 1 The focus of the first group session was to establish cohesion among group members and to encourage group members to begin to discuss their incest experiences. Activities included introductory remarks by the therapist (e.g. acknowledgement of tension and anxiety, comments on common themes related to incest), an activity in which each participant interviewed another participant and introduced her 'partner' to the group, beginning discussion of the incest experience by group members, specification of goals by each participant, and identification of one positive thing participants could do for themselves prior to the next group.

Session 2 The goals of the second group session were to strengthen group cohesion and to further refine or specify goals. Activities included the processing of members' reactions to the prior group, a discussion of the incest literature that had been given out during the intake session, and the circulation of participants' names, addresses, and phone numbers to encourage out-of-group contact between members.

Session 3   Addressing issues of secrecy and isolation was the goal of the third group session. A discussion related to these issues was facilitated first in small groups and then in the larger group. The participants were asked again to identify something positive they could do for themselves during the following week.

Session 4   The goal of this group session was to address the issue of self-esteem and to provide the opportunity for participants to discuss their individual concerns. The participants brainstormed any phrases they associated with the word incest and the leader wrote these phrases on a flip-chart. This procedure was followed by a discussion. In addition, each participant was asked to say something positive about the survivor next to her.

Session 5   The goal of the fifth group session was to address the impact of the incest experience on group participants' current life. Activities included a brainstorming session in which group participants listed children's rights (e.g. control over their bodies, non-sexual physical contact) and needs (e.g. affection, attention). In some of Cole's (1985) groups, members were asked to share with a partner a specific incest incident and then discuss their reactions to this experience with the whole group. The homework assignment following this session was to complete a handout that addressed the stages of healing and had related questions for discussion.

Session 6   The goal of the sixth and final group session was the integration of information. Group members broke up into smaller groups to discuss the questions from the homework handout. Another goal was providing the opportunity for members to say goodbye. Each group member placed a large sheet of paper on the wall and group members wrote a 'positive goodbye message' on each other's paper. Further treatment options (e.g. individual counseling, assertiveness training) were discussed.

Long-term, open-ended groups   A long-term, open-ended, unstructured group allows new members to join the group at any point, does not have a limited number of sessions, and generally does not have a predetermined structure for each group meeting. These groups have also been referred to as non-programmatic groups (Briere, 1989).

There are several advantages and disadvantages to this group format (Hall and Lloyd, 1989). With an open format, members typically have immediate access to the group and greater freedom to leave the group if it is not meeting their needs. New members can keep the group 'fresh' and older members can provide support for newer members. As survivors repeatedly reveal their experience, the secrecy surrounding the abuse is lessened. However, in an open-ended group, newer members may feel excluded whereas older members may be reluctant to continually share their experiences. Intra-group conflicts and breaches of confidentiality are more common. Joining a group without an identified ending point can be threatening for some survivors (Sgroi, 1989b).

Blake-White and Kline (1985) described an incest survivors' group conducted in a mental health center. This group is discussed here as an example of an open-ended, long-term group. An open-ended group was chosen at this setting so that survivors could join when they were ready to do so, rather than waiting for a new group to begin. A long-term format was used, so survivors could explore their issues in depth. There were no specified topics for each session although participants were encouraged to describe their incest experiences. The group leaders described themselves as 'non-directive,' but did indicate that they would encourage the group to focus on one or two issues a session. The leaders would assist members to reframe childhood misperceptions regarding the abuse, express feelings, and make connections between present behaviors and the abuse experience. Because members were at different stages in the healing process, the authors reported that newer members found hope in the progress of others and were able to accept confrontation from survivors who had 'been there.'

Time-limited, consecutive groups   Some group programs combine elements of both the short-term and the long-term formats. Sgroi (1989b), for example, described a series of time-limited survivors' groups conducted by two female co-therapists at a private child abuse treatment center. These groups are discussed here as an example of an alternative format to either the strictly long-term or the strictly short-term group.

Three groups, each running from ten to twelve weeks, are conducted at the center each year. Survivors may choose to participate in one, two, or all of the groups. A commitment to a time-limited group, with an identified stopping point, is experienced by some survivors as less threatening, and more under their control, than an open-ended group. However, having consecutively run groups gives survivors the option to continue with group treatment by joining another group 'cycle' if they desire to do so.

A theme (e.g. dealing with fear, exercising control) is determined for each group. A screening process, which is based on several criteria (e.g. stabilization of acting-out behaviors, ability to discuss victimization experiences) is used. Co-therapist tasks include both attending to the personal treatment needs of each group member (e.g. identification of present coping mechanisms) and facilitating the group process. Group techniques include role playing, body sculpting, art therapy, hypnotic storytelling, and the use of metaphors.

Issues involved in planning a survivors' group

When running a clinical group for survivors of childhood sexual abuse, there are several issues for counselors to consider. These include deciding on the number of sessions, choosing facilitators, determining group composition, choosing a group format, and planning group time. Facilitators should also consider how to handle member screening issues, group ground rules, common group issues, and termination.

Determining the number of sessions

For a short-term structured group, facilitators need to determine how many sessions the group will run. This decision is based on group goals and available resources. Groups with few sessions (e.g. 6–8) are economical and facilitate 'sharp focus on abuse-related issues' (Briere, 1989: 148), but provide limited opportunities for members to get acquainted with one another and do not allow any issues to be addressed in depth. Longer-running groups (e.g. over 12 sessions) allow members to explore issues in more depth, to develop cohesion, and to work on 'abuse-related interpersonal problems' (Briere, 1989: 148), but issues can arise similar to those that occur in open-ended groups, such as the focus on interpersonal conflict rather than on a sexual abuse issue.

Counselors who have run survivors' groups have made recommendations regarding the optimal number of sessions for the short-term group. Cole, for example, stated:

> A six week model, an eight week model and a twelve week model were all tried. The six week model was the most used, due to availability of staff. However, the eight and twelve week models were preferable in giving the clients more opportunity for exploring issues. In the twelve week format transference issues were more apparent as was conflict between group members. (1985: 80)

Briere reached a similar conclusion:

> Although the optimal number of sessions may thus vary according to

the goals of treatment, as well as the setting in which therapy is taking place, the author has found that 10 to 12 sessions (the average number cited in the abuse group literature) is often most effective – allowing enough time for group cohesion to occur, and yet not so extended that intra-group conflicts and habitually dysfunctional behaviors supersede abuse-related concerns. (1989: 148)

Choice of facilitators

Facilitators of survivors' groups should have expertise with abuse issues and skills in group leadership. It is helpful to have at least two counselors facilitate the groups. Survivor groups typically elicit painful material and intense affect and co-facilitators can provide support for one another. Discussing the dynamics of the group following each session can be especially helpful. Two facilitators can also share leadership tasks. For example, if one facilitator is focusing on the needs of an individual group member, the other may attend to group process. Co-facilitators must develop trust and good communication with each other. Supervision is helpful to address any issues that arise in their working relationship.

The gender mix of the co-facilitator team is another issue that has been discussed by counselors who run survivors' groups. Although some counselors suggest that a mixed-gender co-facilitator team for a woman's survivor group may have some advantages (e.g. providing opportunities for members to develop a healthy relationship with a male), two female facilitators may be more likely to enhance trust early in the group process. Cole, for example, maintains that women's survivors' groups should be facilitated by women only:

> Female group leaders decrease the chances of revictimization of the client. Male therapists may quite inadvertently revictimize incest survivors due to their own male enculturation and clients' lack of knowledge and skill in setting emotional and physical boundaries with men. Sexually abused women have been trained to cast males in a dominant and controlling role, which sets the stage for revictimization. The frequently used male and female group leadership team, with its assumption of two positive sex role models, is well beyond the needs of these groups. A pivotal task of these groups centers around creation of trust. The least threatening place to start seems to be trust building with women. Trust in men seems to come later. (1985: 81)

Bruckner and Johnson discussed their recommendations regarding the optimal gender mix of the co-facilitator team for a male survivor group:

> We found it difficult to choose the makeup of the co-facilitator team. From our work with women's support groups, we felt that two facilitators or a mixed-gender team would be more effective. Based on

participants' reports, a minority of women's group participants found it very difficult to disclose and reveal their feelings openly with a male facilitator present. No male participants reported heightened discomfort with a female present. However, they expressed interest in the female therapist's reaction to discussion about current sexual behaviors. They seemed to need her acceptance and permission. Based on our work with male groups, we feel that a female co-facilitator helps reduce discomfort while allowing participants to practice disclosure with both sexes. (1987: 87)

Group composition

Facilitators of survivors' groups must determine the composition of group membership. For example, some groups limit membership to those individuals who were sexually abused, whereas other groups may also include members who were physically or emotionally abused. Many counselors believe that survivors of all types of abuse may experience similar issues and profit from sharing their experiences with other survivors. Gil, who conducts such mixed groups, states:

> This [a mixed group] works well as long as there are an approximately equal number of victims of each type of abuse. The only mixed group that is difficult to conduct is one in which most of the clients were abused in one way, while one or two were abused in another way (for example, eight victims of incest and one victim of physical abuse). This tends to split the group. It also encourages the minority members to feel isolated, misunderstood, and undeserving of help. (1990: 204)

On the other hand, groups with only survivors of childhood sexual abuse may be preferable for dealing specifically with issues of shame and sexuality because sexual abuse survivors have been subjected to activities that are especially taboo in our society and that usually interfere significantly with psychosexual development. Also, feelings of isolation are probably best addressed in a group composed entirely of sexual abuse survivors.

Groups may include both male and female survivors or may be limited to one gender. Mixed-gender groups do have the advantage of helping survivors appreciate the universality of the victimization experience. However, due to issues of trust and the divergent ways in which female and male survivors may express the abuse sequelae, separate gender groups, at least for the initial group experience, may be preferable. Briere (1989) suggested, however, that other 'mixes' of clients (e.g. age, race, sexual orientation, diagnosis) will do well together in groups, although it may be important to balance some client traits (e.g. verbal versus less verbal members).

Group format
The different types of group format (short-term, closed, and structured versus long-term, open-ended, and unstructured) were discussed above. When planning a survivors' group, counselors should consider the benefits and drawbacks of each type of group, the needs of the individuals they hope to serve, and the resources available to them. For example, the long-term, open-ended group may meet the needs of clients whose functioning level is so seriously impaired that it is impossible for them to develop trust within the short-term format. Community mental health agencies may be more likely to serve these survivors and may have the resources to sustain a long-term group. For other survivors, who have identified a very specific, abuse-related goal (e.g. to share their experience with other survivors), a short-term, structured group would be more appropriate. Short-term groups may also be more consistent with the available resources of some agencies (e.g. a counseling center utilizing brief therapy).

Planning group time
Regardless of the basic format of the group, facilitators will need to make some decisions on how group time may be utilized. Hall and Lloyd (1989) have identified three approaches counselors may take to planning the use of group time.

One approach is to introduce certain common topics or themes for discussion at the beginning of each session. This will serve to focus the group meetings and to increase survivors' sense of universality as they realize that others struggle with many of the same issues they do. In structured groups, facilitators often identify these themes in advance. In unstructured groups, facilitators identify issues and themes that have arisen during prior group discussions and help the group focus more specifically on one of these. Examples of themes that might be discussed in groups include:

issues concerning responsibility for the abuse;
the dynamics of the incestuous family;
the prevalence of childhood sexual abuse in society;
the impact of the abuse on members' current relationships;
handling abuse-related effects (e.g. post-traumatic symptoms, guilt, low self-esteem);
interacting with families of origin (e.g. whether or not to confront the offender or non-offending family members);
planning ways to care for oneself;
'moving on' (e.g. forgiveness, finding meaning in the experience, giving up the survivor identity, helping others).

Planned group exercises, another approach to the use of group time, can serve several purposes. Activities can be used to have members address issues experientially, to foster group cohesion, or to practice skills. As discussed above, short-term, structured groups are often based on several of these exercises, planned by facilitators prior to the beginning of the group. Open-ended unstructured groups often incorporate such activities as group needs dictate. For example, if several members are having difficulty appreciating their 'childlikeness' at the time of the abuse, facilitators may introduce an exercise in which members are asked to bring in childhood photos.

Some group activities that have been used in survivor groups include:

1 having group members draw pictures of their families, themselves as children, or the scene where the abuse took place to encourage the non-verbal expression of feelings, to facilitate feedback among group members, and to retrieve memories (Hall and Lloyd, 1989);
2 planning a shared activity, often a common meal or a recreational activity (e.g. a visit to a museum) or engaging in a task requiring cooperation (e.g. designing an anti-abuse poster) to enhance group cohesion;
3 brainstorming (i.e. asking group members to spontaneously generate thoughts that are then written on a large sheet of paper) to facilitate discussion of certain themes or to create a sense of universality. For example, a group may brainstorm any engagement strategies that they could think of that offenders use to gain victims' cooperation. This activity would address the responsibility issue of compliance (i.e. 'He didn't use force, so I must have wanted it');
4 listing strengths and weaknesses or negative self-perceptions that members hold about themselves. These lists are shared with the group and feedback is given to address self-esteem issues and cognitive distortions;
5 discussing literature that was read by all group members to facilitate discussion of specific themes (e.g., Herman's, 1981, work on the three 'discoveries' of incest);
6 participating in skill enhancement activities (e.g. assertiveness training, parent training, relaxation training) to address current abuse-related problems.

A third way group time may be used is referred to as individual time (Hall and Lloyd, 1989). Individual group members are given the opportunity to discuss a pertinent current concern or past issue and to receive feedback from the group. Facilitators afford all members individual time and monitor group member response to the individual who is speaking.

In addition to these approaches, facilitators often choose to discuss group process issues related to interpersonal events among members or between members and facilitators (e.g. conflict, dependency). These issues tend to be more salient in long-term groups. Addressing them can facilitate smoother group functioning and assist members in dealing with interpersonal issues that often bring them to the group initially.

Facilitators may utilize several different methods to begin and end group meetings. Sessions may be opened with a 'check-in' with each member to see how he or she is doing (Gil, 1990), a review of the last meeting, or a sharing of recent achievements (Hall and Lloyd, 1989). Similarly, sessions may be closed with a 'check-in' with each member to see if he or she is feeling distressed or unsafe (Hall and Lloyd, 1989), a summary of the events of the group, or a confirmation of the agenda for the next group meeting. Some facilitators also choose to give homework assignments such as journal keeping or reading related to the aspect of the childhood abuse that was discussed in the group session.

Screening
A meeting with facilitators prior to group involvement gives survivors the opportunity to meet the facilitators and for the facilitators to share the format, structure, and ground rules of the group with interested survivors. A primary purpose of this meeting can be screening survivors for appropriateness for group membership. This agenda should be made clear to potential group members and any decision on group involvement should be mutually determined after a discussion of the survivors' goals and the group's purpose.

Group facilitators often develop membership criteria. If survivors exhibit problems that limit their ability to participate fully in a group or that may result in disruption of the group, they are often referred for individual therapy or for other appropriate services (e.g. hospitalization, substance abuse treatment programs). Exclusionary criteria may include:

psychosis or disorientation;
active suicidality;
excessive hostility or aggressiveness;
current abuse of drugs or alcohol;
an inability to discuss the abuse experience to any extent with the screener.

Briere (1989) cautioned facilitators against using strict exclusion criteria, some of which reflect typical long-term effects of abuse (i.e. suicidality). Using these criteria automatically eliminates many survivors who request group treatment. He suggested that facilitators evaluate the *extent* of each survivor's problem (e.g. distinguishing active suicidal intent from passing suicidal thoughts) and the *degree* to which these problems would actually interfere with group involvement.

Membership criteria are also often dependent on other factors, such as the setting in which the group is run. For example, some in-patient facilities provide intensive group therapy for survivors who are acutely suicidal because they can be closely monitored for any self-destructive behavior that is exacerbated by group participation. Community groups are unable to provide such support and therefore often screen out actively suicidal survivors.

The screening meeting can also be used as a first goal-setting session in which facilitators can determine if the survivor's goals are appropriate for the format of the group being run. For example, to share one's abuse experience with other survivors or to receive feedback from others regarding responsibility issues would be appropriate goals for a short-term group. However, to learn to trust others, when one has never done this before, is probably not a realistic goal to accomplish in 6–12 sessions. During the screening process facilitators can either help survivors refine goals that cannot be realistically met given a group's format or refer them to a more appropriate group.

Ground rules and boundaries
It is important for group facilitators to identify and discuss group ground rules. Important ground rules in most groups are related to confidentiality, safety, group time, attendance, and out-of-group contact.

Confidentiality Because trust is a key issue in survivor groups, confidentiality is an important ground rule to address. Facilitators should state the expectation that all material discussed in group will not be shared outside the group. However, facilitators should specify that they cannot guarantee this and it is each member's responsibility to respect other members' confidentiality. If the facilitators share group material with colleagues, for the purpose of consultation, supervision, or collaboration with individual therapists, group members should be informed of this. Limits of confidentiality (e.g. that information suggesting danger to self or others or related to child abuse will be revealed) should also be discussed.

Safety Ground rules related to safety issues should be addressed as well. For example, facilitators should emphasize that the physical safety of members should be respected and that no physical violence will be tolerated in group. Ground rules regarding members' 'emotional safety' can also be important. It is useful, for example, to discuss the differences between a personal verbal attack and helpful confrontation.

Group time Because survivors often struggle with boundary issues, group parameters, such as the starting and stopping times of the sessions, should be clearly specified and maintained. Groups can become emotionally charged toward the designated stopping time, and in these instances it can be tempting to extend group time to obtain closure on issues that may have arisen late in the session. However, if such issues do arise, group facilitators should acknowledge the end of the group and the fact that the group is ending with unfinished business. Regularly extending group time to resolve issues represents a disrespect of the boundaries of the group members and the group facilitators. Instead, facilitators may assist the group in making plans for addressing unfinished issues in another way. For example, a group may agree to begin the next session with the unresolved issue or may help members who are distressed at the end of a group plan how they can take care of themselves or meet their safety needs until the group next meets.

Attendance Expectations regarding group attendance should be addressed. While members of some support groups are not expected to attend all groups, most clinical group facilitators request that members attend group regularly and contact the facilitator if they are unable to attend any session.

Facilitators of short-term groups typically ask members to commit to all sessions before beginning the group. Similarly, facilitators of long-term, open-ended groups often ask survivors to commit to a certain number of sessions (e.g. four) in order to give the group a 'fair try.' This discourages survivors from fleeing after an initial session due to anxiety or shame related to exposure. It is helpful to discuss the desire to leave the group and feeling of being trapped in the group by such commitments. However, if a survivor nonetheless chooses to leave the group, this decision should be respected. Some facilitators may request that the survivor share with the group the reasons for his or her choice to leave. This helps to decrease other members' feelings of rejection or abandonment and gives the departing group member a sense of closure.

Out-of-group contact Contact between group sessions, both among members and between a member and a facilitator, is another issue to discuss with group members. As mentioned previously, some group facilitators actively encourage group members to have contact with each other between sessions as it is believed that this can decrease survivor isolation (Cole, 1985). However, there are some disadvantages to this practice. If survivors have not yet dealt with issues of personal boundaries, assertiveness, and limit setting, they can feel overwhelmed if another group member calls them in distress or begins to depend on them for support. The advantages and disadvantages of out-of-group contact can be addressed and members can be encouraged to make their own choices regarding sharing phone numbers and addresses.

Out-of-group contact with facilitators is also an issue to address at the beginning of a group. Some facilitators believe their availability between sessions enables survivors to feel safe and supported. Others discourage between-session contact to avoid having members deal individually with issues best discussed in group. As out-of-group contacts can represent boundary issues, the facilitators' policy on this should be clearly defined. Regardless, plans should be made to meet group members' individual and emergency counseling needs as they arise during group involvement. This can be accomplished by requiring members to have continuing contact with an individual therapist or by providing access to a crisis service (e.g. a hotline, an emergency service facility).

Common group issues

Several of the issues that frequently arise in survivor groups typically require facilitator intervention. Although any number of approaches can be used when these issues arise, some suggested counselor interventions are outlined here.

Resistance
As the issue of childhood sexual abuse can be so difficult to share with others, group members often exhibit resistance to group participation. Because of anxiety precipitated by the group experience, members may miss sessions, come late for sessions, or forget to complete homework assignments. Counselor interventions that may be used to address behaviors related to resistance include the following:

Confront the behavior (e.g. absence from sessions) in a non-judgmental manner.

Encourage resistant survivors to describe their group experiences (e.g. what it was like for them to disclose the abuse) in order to begin to identify their anxiety.

Respond empathically to pain experienced by the resistant survivor as the result of group involvement.

Assist the survivor to connect the resistant behavior with his or her anxiety.

Ask other group members (a) to give feedback to the resistant member regarding how they are affected by his or her behavior; and (b) to share their ways of handling the anxiety they experience as a group member.

In the following interaction, both group members and the facilitator confront a survivor's resistance, which was evidenced by her missing several sessions following the disclosure of her abuse experience.

Counselor: Polly, I've noticed you've missed the last two sessions.

Jane: Ya, where have you been Polly?

June: Yes, everyone was asking about you.

Jane: We missed you.

June: You agreed to come to all the sessions.

Gretchen: Last time you were here you were so upset. We worried about you.

Polly: Really, it's no big deal, OK. I'll come from now on. For heaven's sake, I'm OK.

Counselor: What is it like to hear that other group members missed you and were concerned about you?

Polly: I was afraid everyone would make a fuss like this. I was embarrassed the last time I was here. I never cry like that. I shouldn't have said what I did about my father. I really didn't want everyone worrying about me.

Counselor: It was not only hard, then, for you to disclose your abuse and to experience the feelings that resulted from that, but it was also hard to have others show caring and concern for you.

Polly: Well, I'm certainly not used to it. My husband couldn't have cared less when I told him about what happened to me. You'd think I'd like people fussing about me, but it makes me uncomfortable.

Counselor: Has anyone else experienced anything similar to this?

Jane: Yes, I missed a lot of group sessions at first too. It was hard to face everyone. I just stayed away. Now, I never miss.

Counselor: What is different for you now?

Jane: I think I just feel more comfortable here. Polly will too if she just sticks it out. You have to force yourself to come. Then you learn everyone really means well.

Counselor: Yes, sharing experiences and feelings is not easy, especially when you are used to others ignoring those feelings. As you have

pointed out, Jane, you missed sessions rather than face sharing with the group.
Jane: Ya, but you have to hang in there.
Polly: I'll try. That's why I am here tonight.

Silence

Some members attend group regularly but consistently remain silent. When this occurs, counseling interventions may include the following:

Confront the silence in a non-judgmental manner.
Ask silent group members to describe their group experiences.
Assist silent group members in connecting their silence to anxiety, problems with trust, or low self-esteem (i.e. their feeling that what they have to say is not valuable, or even 'stupid').
Ask other members to share any reluctance they have had about speaking in group.
Encourage silent members to slowly begin to risk sharing their experiences and reactions with the group.

In the following interaction, a group member's silence is addressed.

Janice: You know, April, it's been three weeks and you haven't said a word. I wonder what you are thinking sometimes.
April: I really haven't had anything to say.
Janice: Everyone else said something about guilt [that day's topic].
April: I'll try to come up with something next time. I really can't think of anything right now. Sorry.
Counselor: Sometimes it's hard to speak up in group. Has anyone else had problems at any point sharing their thoughts or feelings here?
Dodie: I did at first. I thought everyone would laugh at me.
Susan: Me, too. It seemed like everyone knew each other and said all these insightful things.
Joan: I was used to everyone, you know, my family, telling me to shut up. I came here and I'm supposed to speak up?
Dodie: That's it. We're used to keeping secrets. Here we tell really private things. It's hard.
Counselor: So there are many reasons why it's hard to talk here. You may fear others will laugh or find out you're stupid. You may have gotten the message from others outside of the group to be quiet or to keep secrets. Are any of these things similar to what you've experienced, April?
April: Yes, the sounding stupid part.
Joan: Believe me, you won't sound stupid. We've all gone through similar stuff. We won't laugh at you.
April: I never spoke up in school, either. I was dumb there.
Joan: Me too. But group is different. When you're ready, we would really like to hear what you have to say.

Hostility

Hostility expressed by group members is a particularly important issue to address, as safety issues are paramount in survivors' groups. When anger is expressed in a destructive way toward group members (e.g. threats, verbal abuse, name-calling) facilitators should model 'protective responses' (Gil, 1990: 237). Counselors may use the following interventions:

Clearly define unacceptable hostile behaviors and restrict these behaviors in group.
Discuss the difference between hostility, which is distancing in relationships, and the constructive expression of anger, which can enhance relationships.
Facilitate the appropriate expression of anger.
Ask other group members to describe (a) their response to the hostile behavior; and (b) the ways they handle their own anger in the group.

In the following interaction, one group member's expressed hostility to another is addressed:

Susy: Don't tell me that you understand what I feel. I'm sick to death of your garbage. Always having an opinion about my life when your life is such a mess. Frankly, I wish you would stop being a busybody or a shrink and leave me alone.
Jacqueline: Sorry, I was just trying to help.
Counselor: Susy – one ground rule we have established in this group is that no one can verbally attack anyone else. If you are angry at Jacqueline you can tell her that, but you cannot call her names nor put down her ideas or her feedback.
Susy: She's always on my case and I'm sick of it.
Counselor: Would you tell Jacqueline how you feel and what you would like from her without putting her down?
Susy: Alright. Alright. I get angry when you tell me what to do all the time. I will leave my husband when I'm ready. Just listen to me. Don't give me advice.

Monopolizing the group

Some members may tend to monopolize the group. One example of this is the group member who has multiple problems that he or she brings to group each week. Counseling interventions to address this issue include the following:

Confront the behavior in a non-judgmental manner.
Set limits on the behavior.
Support other members in providing constructive feedback.
Assist the survivor in connecting his or her behavior with

anxiety, problems with boundaries and control, or an excessive need for attention (Gil, 1990).
Facilitate a group discussion regarding how to meet needs for attention in ways that do not distance others.

In the following interaction, Jim, a group member who tends to monopolize the group, is confronted by other group members and the group facilitator.

> *Jim:* I would like to discuss a fight I had with my wife. You see, I was late coming home on Wednesday . . . .
> *Peter:* Come on, Jim. All last week we talked about you and your wife. Jeff, here, confronted his brother [the offender] and we haven't even heard how that went.
> *Jim:* Sorry, I thought we were supposed to say what's on our minds. Go ahead, Jeff. I won't say another word.
> *Counselor:* Let's talk about what happened between Jim and Peter and then I know I would like to hear from Jeff as well. What was Peter's feedback like for you, Jim?
> *Jim:* Well, I know I talk a lot. I didn't like to hear it, though. I was a little angry. I think anyone would be. I guess I know I turn others off sometimes.
> *Counselor:* Peter, what was it like for you to give the feedback?
> *Peter:* I didn't want to hurt his feelings, but I think we should all have more time to talk. It was hard to be the one to say something.
> *Counselor:* So it was hard for you to say and hard for Jim to hear. And yet we are here to give and receive feedback. Let's talk about how we use 'air time' in the group. Usually, members who use a lot of 'air time' are needing something from the group. Jim, could you talk about what you might need from the group now?
> *Jim:* I guess this is the only place people listen to me. My wife doesn't, my family doesn't.
> *Counselor:* How might you meet your need to be heard in this group without using too much 'air time,' which, as you say, can turn others off?

Termination

Regardless of the format of the group, termination is always a significant group issue. In structured groups, activities are often planned to assist survivors in reviewing their group experiences, in saying goodbye to other members, in dealing with feelings of loss, and in planning future courses of action. In open-ended groups, the issues are dealt with as each individual chooses to end his or her involvement with the group.

Briere (1989) identified three important principles related to termination in survivor groups. First, the termination date is specified well in advance of the final meeting. Second, group members are frequently reminded that group participation, even if long term, is for a finite period. This allows all members to prepare for termination throughout their group experience. Finally, the final group sessions should be 'ceremonialized,' so that survivors have the opportunity to experience closure and say goodbye.

In the following interaction, the group facilitator encourages group members to deal with their feelings of loss. The interaction takes place following a party that members had planned for the final session of a 12-week survivor group.

Sharon: Well, this is over. It really wasn't so bad. I thought I would hate coming and then I ended up !ooking forward to it.

Counselor: What about the group will you miss?

Sharon: Just coming here, having someone to talk to. I never told anyone what was done to me. I'll miss this group on Tuesday nights.

Counselor: Does anyone else have similar feelings?

June: I do. It's like I just got to know everyone and now I will not see you all any more.

Darlene: I felt kind of sad coming tonight. I almost stayed home.

Tanya: I wonder what I will do with myself on Tuesdays. I feel like you are my friends. I know some of us will keep in touch, but not everyone. You know, we say we will meet for coffee but we probably won't.

Counselor: So it is important to say goodbye tonight.

Tanya: Yes. You know you tell people you'll see them around and you know you won't.

Counselor: Saying 'I'll see you later' is really avoiding saying goodbye, which can be very hard.

Tanya: Now you're going to make me cry. I've only known you all a few months and yet I've never felt closer to any other women.

Terry: I think it's because we all went through something similar.

Darlene: Yes, many of my friends know I was abused, but this is different. They really don't understand like you all did.

Counselor: So you will be saying goodbye tonight to others who you feel very close to in a special way. Are there particular things you would like to say to each other?

Tanya: I want to tell Terry I appreciated the time she held my hand when I was crying about my mother leaving me . . . .

Case Study: The Counseling Process with an Adult Survivor of Childhood Sexual Abuse

This chapter summarizes some of the counseling principles that have been discussed by describing the counseling experience of Sue, an adult survivor who sought counseling at a community agency, from intake to termination. Sue was in individual counseling for approximately a year and a half. This was her first counseling experience.

Background

Sue was a 44-year-old female who sought counseling for complaints of general life dissatisfaction and concern related to her drinking habits. She was living with her mother who was 76 years old and in poor health due to long-standing heart problems. Sue reported that she had been 'taking care' (e.g. shopping, housekeeping, arranging doctor's visits) of her mother for many years, but described their relationship as strained and conflict ridden. She claimed her mother was very 'cranky' and would usually complain that Sue was not doing things 'right.' At times, Sue resented having her mother depend on her. Sue's father and mother had been separated for approximately forty years. Her father lived in a distant state. Sue would call him periodically, but would usually find him drunk when she called. She claimed to have little memory of her father because he left the family when she was four years old.

Sue had two older sisters and one younger brother. Her sisters were both married and living in another state. They visited infrequently, usually during the holidays. Sue stated that her younger brother, John, had 'emotional problems' and was currently living in a nearby rooming house. When he ran out of money, he would sometimes return to live with Sue and her mother. According to Sue, this arrangement would usually be problematic as John was 'difficult to control' and would sometimes become violent. Although he did not attack Sue or her mother, he would destroy their belongings (e.g. smash dishes, break furniture). Sue stated that he would also get drunk, steal from the family, and stay away for days at a time. Sue's mother would insist that Sue 'keep an eye' on John when he stayed with them.

Sue was employed as the receptionist and secretary for a small local industry. She had been at her job for over twenty years, since graduating from high school. Although she was reluctant to 'compliment herself,' Sue did indicate that her work was highly regarded by her employer. She had not missed a day of work since she was hired. Although her work could be monotonous at times, she basically enjoyed her job and her relationship with her few co-workers.

Sue reported that after work she would usually stop at a local restaurant for dinner and a few drinks before coming home to watch television, when she would have a few more drinks. She stated that she had no friends outside of work other than Jim, a young man who lived in the apartment above hers. She described him as a 'shy loner – much like me.' Jim would suggest from time to time that they get married, but Sue denied any interest in Jim that was 'more than friends.' Their relationship did not include sexual intimacy. Sue reported that she had always been relatively isolated from anyone outside her family.

Assessing a history of childhood sexual abuse

Sue did not come for an intake session for several months after her initial call to the agency, as she broke several scheduled appointments. On some of these occasions, she claimed that she had to take her mother to a doctor's appointment.

When Sue finally did attend a scheduled appointment, she told the counselor that she was very anxious. She stated, 'I never thought I would be the type of person to do this [seek counseling].' She began by describing herself as a 'plain Jane old maid.' Sue revealed that she got up one morning and realized that she was unhappy with her life and did not want to 'live the next 20 years like I lived that last 20.' However, she was unable to articulate what changes she wanted to make in her life other than wanting to 'get out more with people.' She did report that she had completely stopped drinking over two months ago when she made the call for her initial counseling appointment.

During the second session, Sue appeared very anxious and avoided eye contact with the counselor. She began the session by stating, 'I think I had better tell you about some weird dreams I've been having.' Sue then revealed that she had several dreams in which she was a little girl and was in bed with her father. She experienced these dreams as very frightening. She stated that she feared that having these 'dirty' dreams suggested that she was 'some kind of pervert.' In the following interaction, Sue discusses her dreams and she and the counselor explore the possibility that the dreams reflect a sexual abuse experience she may have had as a child.

> *Sue:* I think it's strange I would have such a weird dream. I mean my father, for God's sake. That's bizarre. I must be some kind of weirdo. I wasn't just in bed with him. It was like, well, sexual. He was touching me where he shouldn't be, you know, my private parts. The dreams are fuzzy, that's all I can remember.
>
> *Counselor:* What do the dreams mean to you?
>
> *Sue:* It's just bizarre. I know people have weird dreams but this is too strange. You must think I'm perverted.
>
> *Counselor:* No, I don't. People can have dreams like this for any number of reasons. I can see it was hard for you to tell me about these dreams, however. I respect your courage for bringing them up.
>
> *Sue:* You don't think this actually happened, you know, in real life?
>
> *Counselor:* Dreams may sometimes reflect incidents that happened in childhood that were too painful to remember. Is it possible that your father did sleep with you and fondle you when you were a child?
>
> *Sue:* You mean that my father actually molested me? That was my first thought also – but no – it can't be. I would remember that, I'm sure. My father was a drunk when he lived with us. He was violent. He never beat us girls, but he did beat my mother occasionally and my brother often. But have sex with me? I sure don't remember anything like that happening. No, that I would remember because it would be so disgusting. The dreams seemed so real though. It is a strange experience. I'm all mixed up.
>
> *Counselor:* Yes, these dreams are confusing to you. May I ask you some other questions regarding experiences you may have had that might be related in some way to your dreams?
>
> *Sue:* Please do.
>
> *Counselor:* Have you ever had other experiences, maybe even when you are awake, that felt strange or unreal to you?
>
> *Sue:* Well, yes, sometimes. Even when I'm awake I sometimes feel there is someone in my room. Is that the kind of thing you mean? I've always felt that was strange. I don't see things, mind you, I just feel something. Like a sensation. Now you are going to think I'm really weird.
>
> *Counselor:* No, I don't think that. Many people have such experiences that are hard to explain, but that does not mean they are weird. In fact, I'd like to hear more about these sensations.

Discussion

Sue's initial presentation was consistent with a possible undisclosed history of sexual abuse. She presented with two symptoms common to sexual abuse survivors: social isolation and substance abuse. In addition, she also described a history of parentification in which she had cared for a sickly mother from a young age. As an adult, she continued to take care of her mother and her troubled brother. Her father was described as impulsive, violent, and chemically dependent. Sue also revealed a more specific, and therefore more predictive, symptom of a recurring nightmare in which her father was fondling her. She experienced this dream as frightening and confusing.

Because of these factors, a more in-depth assessment was carried out. This included a mental status exam covering the thought and perceptual disturbances that are thought to be characteristic of a sexual abuse history (Ellenson, 1985). Sue revealed experiencing illusions of a presence in her room and tactile hallucinations, the feeling that her body was being touched. In response to the counselor's direct inquiry regarding a sexual abuse experience in her childhood, Sue revealed that she had considered that she might have been molested by her father, but had ruled out this possibility because she had no memories of any actual abuse incidents. After several more recurrences of the nightmare, however, Sue grew more and more convinced that some abuse had actually occurred. Due to Sue's conviction that she had been abused, her clinical presentation, and her family history, her counseling proceeded on the assumption that she very likely had experienced sexual abuse as a child.

Focus on the abuse experience

Sue continued to have nightmares in which she, as a child, was in bed with her father as he fondled her genitals. Shortly after revealing that she had accepted the 'reality' of the abuse, she frequently began to miss counseling appointments. When confronted with this, Sue told the counselor that she was concerned that if she continued to discuss the abuse she would begin drinking again. She also expressed the belief that delving into the possibility that her father had abused her was not related to her current concerns. She questioned how significant the abuse really was if she had not remembered it. Therefore, while she acknowledged the abuse experience, she did initially minimize its importance. However, Sue comes to consider that the abuse might have an impact on her current problems in the following interaction with the counselor.

Sue: I'm 44. I'm lonely. I've stopped drinking and yet I'm still miserable. Now, on top of this, I've discovered my dad was a dirty old man who messed with me. Knowing this has not helped me. In fact, it's made me more anxious. I still have the problem I came here with. I'm alone and I don't know what to do about it. I've learned the abuse happened, but for what? For nothing?

Counselor: I know that coming to realize your dad abused you has been difficult. You have experienced more anxiety, more nightmares. And yet you have endured this without drinking. However, I do not believe it has been for nothing. So often, an abusive experience like the one you suffered as a child is related to adult problems.

Sue: How can this be? As nearly as I can figure out, it happened almost forty years ago.

Counselor: Well, for example, being sexually abused as a young child by a parent can affect how the child relates to others when he or she grows up. Or the way the child learns to cope with the abuse continues to be the way he or she copes with things as an adult . . . .

Sue: Like – I always hid out in my room as a kid. Now I know I was probably trying to get away from what was happening. I played alone for hours and had no friends. I still hide out in my room now in a way.

Discussion

In this interaction, the counselor suggested a possible connection between the abuse and Sue's current difficulties. For Sue, making the connection between hiding out in her room as a child and 'hiding out' as an adult was a powerful experience. If she had not made a connection between the abuse and her current concerns she probably would not have chosen to continue to deal with the abuse issue in counseling. Once she made this connection, and thereby ceased to minimize the abuse, she contracted with the counselor to focus on the abuse experience as a way of understanding her current difficulties.

Retrieval of memories

Although her nightmares had become quite vivid, Sue desired more 'evidence' to counteract a nagging doubt that she was 'making the whole thing up.' The counselor and she planned to use some techniques to retrieve memories of the abuse or to validate Sue's suspicions that the abuse had occurred. This became the focus of much of Sue's counseling.

Before attempting memory retrieval, the counselor discussed with Sue the possibility that this process might be accompanied initially by an increase in symptomatology (e.g. nightmares). The counselor also indicated that this increase was a temporary, and at times necessary, part of the healing process. The risk of Sue resuming alcohol use to deal with these symptoms or to deal with the pain of exploring the abuse was also a concern. Sue considered, but rejected, the recommendation that she utilize Alcoholics Anonymous as an adjunct support during this time. She did remain sober throughout her counseling experience.

Several counseling techniques were used to assist Sue in memory retrieval. Discussing general childhood memories proved helpful. For example, when Sue talked about her mother's preoccupation with health issues, the counselor inquired as to what impact this had had on Sue as a child. Sue revealed that her mother took her to the doctor for even the most minor ailments. When Sue was describing an incident in which her mother took her to a doctor when she had her first menstrual period, Sue remembered that the doctor had told her mother that Sue must have fallen off her bike as she had injuries 'down there.' Sue felt confused about this because at the time she had not remembered having any such accident. She had been concerned that her mother might have thought that she had had sex at school, but her mother never mentioned the doctor's visit again. Looking back, Sue concluded that the vaginal injuries were likely to have been the result of sexual abuse and that her mother did not respond to the doctor's revelation because she did not want to deal with what Sue's father had done.

To further memory retrieval, the counselor recommended that Sue bring in an old family photograph taken at a time when she was a very young child. Sue found only one old photo of her family. In the photo, she was in the first grade. Sue asked her mother if there were other photos and her mother told her that the family themselves had never owned a camera and that the photograph Sue had found was taken by her grandmother. Although the photograph did not produce memories of abuse incidents, it did provoke several fruitful discussions about Sue's family. While viewing the photo, Sue discussed her father's alcoholism and the severe physical abuse of her brother by her father, much of which Sue had witnessed. She also revealed that her mother did not 'seem to notice' her brother's beatings. As exemplified in the following dialogue, discussing these family dynamics (her father's poor impulse control; her mother's denial) gave Sue a greater appreciation of the ways in which her family was at risk for incest:

Sue: You know you can tell something is wrong with this family even by looking at this photo. No one is smiling. You know how families always smile in pictures. We all look miserable. No wonder we never had our own camera. Look at my brother. He looks mad! No wonder. My father beats him and my mother couldn't care less.
Counselor: What do you think when you look at yourself in the picture?
Sue: I look dumb, I think. We all look weird. Other families stand close to each other or touch each other. We look wooden. My father even

looks mean; my mother looks frail. I look spaced out.
Counselor: Spaced out?
Sue: Ya, like not there. I have such a blank look.
Counselor: What do you make of that?
Sue: It's like I checked out. I don't look happy. I don't look sad. I just
look there. That's how I felt. I was just there. I don't remember
being happy, but I don't remember being sad either. When my father
beat my brother, I think I would kind of pretend that it wasn't
happening. Like I made myself numb.
Counselor: What do you think of when you look at your family as a
whole?
Sue: Looking at this picture I realize this family is not normal. I do see
how I could have been abused and not remember it. My father did
what he wanted, my mother didn't notice, and I was spaced out. Like
I was in a coma.

Perhaps the most powerful experience for Sue in her attempts at
memory retrieval were contacts with her older sisters. Through
discussions with the counselor, Sue had concluded that her sisters
might have had some memories of their father's relationship with
Sue, or might even have been abused themselves by their father.
Sue recalled that both sisters had left home immediately after high
school. Her father had been extremely strict with her oldest sister,
flying into a rage whenever she brought dates home. Sue, who by
this time had read a good deal of material on incestuous families,
concluded that her father's response to her sister's dates reflected
a 'possessive jealousy,' which is often characteristic of a sexually
abusive father.

After much discussion and preparation, Sue decided to contact
her sisters by telephone, disclose her conclusions regarding her
abuse, and ask for their help in retrieving further memories. She
first called Jill, the younger of the two sisters, who denied any
memories of abuse by the father and in fact was quite critical that
Sue would even suggest such a 'dirty-minded' thing. Despite having
considered before making the call that this might have been Jill's
response, Sue nonetheless felt 'devastated' at her sister's reaction
to her disclosure and request for help. (It was later revealed by
Sue's mother that all the girls had in fact been sexually abused by
their father.)

Sue's older sister, Paula, responded quite differently. When Sue
told her the purpose of the call, Paula became very quiet and
started to cry. Paula revealed that she had been abused by their
father from the ages of 10 to 16, when she left home. She stated
that she had hoped that Sue had been spared his abuse, but she had
'always wondered.' During this conversation, Sue and Paula determined that Sue's abuse probably occurred between the time Paula

left home and the time when her father left the family. This would put Sue at about age 3–4, which was the age Sue believed herself to be in her dreams. Paula decided to visit Sue and Sue invited Paula to one of her counseling sessions. Both sisters were very supportive of one another. They were able to cry together and commiserated that they had both suffered, but until now had not been able to share each other's pain.

Discussion

In order for Sue to appreciate the relationship between her current experience and her abuse and to relieve her distressing nightmares, memory retrieval or validation of her suspicions of abuse was important. Preparing for techniques aimed at memory retrieval or validation of the suspected abuse involved planning for the possible consequences of these processes. For Sue, resumption of alcohol use was the most salient concern. As mentioned previously, she refused involvement with AA. Sue had been sober for several months and remained sober throughout her counseling experience. However, this relatively short period of sobriety, and the lack of support that AA or a similar treatment program could provide, may have put Sue at risk of exacerbation of substance abuse during the phases of disclosure and memory retrieval. If chemical dependency is a problem, counselors may choose to make involvement in a substance abuse program and a longer period of sobriety (e.g. a year) a prerequisite of sexual abuse counseling. Although Sue's counselor did not choose this intervention, and Sue remained sober, a stipulation of involvement in chemical dependency treatment may be appropriate.

Several different techniques were used for memory retrieval, including discussion of childhood experiences, use of old photographs, and interactions with siblings. Although Sue's memories of the abuse incidents did not return, her suspicions that the abuse had happened were confirmed. Once this occurred, Sue was able to give up her quest to recall the actual incidents and began to discuss her feelings related to her childhood experiences. At first, she expressed rage towards her father but eventually felt only pity. Sue more frequently discussed her sadness over what was done to her and her sisters when they were 'just little girls.' As she accepted the reality of the incest and discussed her feelings related to her abuse, her nightmares did subside.

Reinterpreting the sexual abuse experience from an adult perspective

Because Sue was abused at such an early age and because her father abused all family members either sexually or physically, Sue began to blame her father, not herself, for the abuse relatively early in the healing process. She therefore did not struggle as intensely with responsibility issues as do some survivors. Following her interactions with her sister, Sue quite clearly stated her belief that her father was a 'very sick man' and that she and her sisters were not to blame for the abuse.

She did deal, however, with the issue of sexual responsiveness, as in her dream she experienced responding sexually to her father. Sue asked, 'I know I was too young to ask for it [the abuse], but did I enjoy it?' When her sexual response was reframed by the counselor as a natural physiological reaction, even for a 3-year old, rather than an indication that she had enjoyed the activity, Sue was able to resolve this issue.

Addressing the context of the sexual abuse

For Sue, addressing the context of the sexual abuse experience was an important issue. Her father's alcoholism and explosive temper and her mother's obsession with the physical health of the family had a significant impact on Sue's childhood development. Sue, who avidly read anything she could get her hands on regarding sexual abuse, did the same for material related to alcoholic families. She identified herself as the 'family hero' (Wegscheider-Cruse, 1985) because she was always the child who did well at school and who had assumed the responsibility of caring for her mother. Sue was able to see how she continued to play these roles as an adult because she continued to be very responsible at work (e.g. never missing a day, 'doing the work of two people') and continued to provide for her mother's, and now her brother's, needs. She recognized that she was unable to meet her own needs and thus had ultimately become very dissatisfied with her life.

Sue was especially interested in the concept of the 'closed family system' (Satir, 1988). Her family's isolation had been profound. Her parents never had friends and discouraged the children from having friends as well. Sue recognized that Paula's attempts at dating, in addition to making her father jealous, had broken a significant unspoken family rule about interacting with 'outsiders.' For this Paula had been punished with her father's rage. Other attempts by the parents to discourage the children from having friends were more subtle. Often the parents would simply 'bad-mouth' any other children Sue or her siblings mentioned. Sue recognized that her isolation as an adult resulted in part from this deep distrust of those outside the family. She also recalled being reluctant to bring home children from school for fear her father would be drinking and violent.

Exploring her mother's role in the abuse was also important to Sue. While she acknowledged the rage she initially felt toward her father she stated that she 'did not know how to feel' toward her mother. After discussing her mother's behavior during Sue's childhood (e.g. pretending not to notice John's beatings; ignoring the doctor's revelation of Sue's 'accident') and considering the young age at which Sue believed the abuse took place, Sue concluded that her mother knew of the abuse but did not intervene. In the following counselor–client interaction, Sue reaches this conclusion and decides to confront her mother. The counselor recommends that Sue plan for this confrontation before carrying it out.

> *Sue:* I can't believe she let this happen. But she must have. She never left the house. I was 3 or 4 years old. How could she not know? When the doctor told her about my 'accident,' she never asked about it again. She must have known what really caused it or she would have asked me about it. Yes, she knew. She just ignored it.
>
> *Counselor:* What has it been like for you to reach this conclusion about your mom?
>
> *Sue:* I don't know. I need to know for sure. Now, I can't feel anything. I mean if I really knew I would be angry. I need to ask her. After everything I've done for her. I was the only one to stick by her. I'm going to ask her when I get home.
>
> *Counselor:* I can see it's important for you to find out for sure whether your mother knew what your father was doing and asking your mom directly of course would be a way to find out. It is usually helpful to plan this ahead – what you will say to your mom, what you hope will happen, what it might feel like for you to do this. That way it feels more in your control.
>
> *Sue:* OK, I won't run home and do it tonight.
>
> *Counselor:* Let's start by discussing what it might be like for you to confront your mom . . . .

Sue recognized that the confrontation in itself would be very difficult for her because she was accustomed to protecting her mom from anything unpleasant and in this instance she would be bringing up a painful issue. She hoped that her mom would confirm what Sue really believed to be true, and that was that her mom knew of the abuse but felt powerless to stop it. Sue knew this would be very hard to hear but would be a 'step in the right direction' toward sorting out her feelings regarding her mother's involvement in the abuse dynamics. Sue also explored her possible reactions if her mother denied knowledge of the abuse. She guessed that if her mother did not 'take responsibility and admit the truth,' Sue would feel very resentful.

Before confronting her mom, Sue practiced exactly what she wanted to say. She decided to begin the conversation with this statement:

> Mom, I now know Dad abused me by having sex with me when I was very little. I do not question that it happened. Would you tell me if you were aware he was doing this to me? It is important to me that I know.

When Sue confronted her mother, her mother did admit that she had known what the father was doing to all the kids (i.e. sexually abusing the girls and physically abusing John). Sue's mother confirmed Sue's belief that she felt powerless to stop the abuse because of the father's violent temper, the family's dependency on his paycheck, and her own 'ill-health.' Sue's mother became very tearful and yet 'somehow calm' as she told Sue that she had hoped that Sue had been too young to realize what was happening to her. Her mother told Sue that one of the reasons Sue's father had left the house when he did was because he was afraid Paula would tell the authorities of her abuse.

Initially, Sue felt enraged with her mother. Sue continually stated that she was very resentful that she had been her mom's caretaker all these years, whereas her mom had not protected her when she was a young child. Eventually, Sue came to appreciate her mother's limitations, which Sue termed her 'extreme weakness of character.' Sue stated that although she did not 'forgive' her mother for not protecting her from the abuse, she did resolve her own feelings toward her mother by coming to understand why her mother did not take action. She was therefore no longer consumed with needing to know what her mother knew about the abuse and felt less bitterness as time went on.

Discussion

Counseling interventions that were aimed at helping Sue explore the context of the abuse included facilitating a discussion related to dysfunctional families. When Sue recognized that she had assumed the role of the responsible, but joyless, child in her family and that the family system in which she grew up was extremely 'closed,' she came to appreciate that her social isolation, her main presenting concern, was in many ways an extension of her family's history. Having this insight freed her to make other choices regarding social relationships as an adult.

Facilitating Sue's exploration of her mother's role in the abuse and helping her plan and process the confrontation were also important counseling interventions. Once Sue was able to confirm what she had suspected about the extent of her mother's knowledge of the abuse and was able to deal with her feelings related to this, she was able to decide what kind of relationship she would like to maintain with her. Sue identified the unhealthy aspects of their relationship and decided to make changes in the way she interacted with her mother. She realized, for example, that many of the things she did for her mother (e.g. arranging doctor's appointments) were things her mother could do for herself. Ultimately, despite protests from her mother, Sue decided to move to her own apartment and was gradually able to give up her caretaking role.

Making desired life changes

Even prior to beginning counseling, Sue had made a major life change: achieving and maintaining sobriety. However, she continued to feel lonely and isolated, often seeing only her mother and brother and the few individuals she worked with in the course of a day. As previously mentioned, she realized that she was continuing a family pattern of social isolation. Sue also recognized that, due to the abuse and the family dynamics that surrounded it, she felt poorly about herself, believing she would have very little to offer if she did make any friends. She often stated 'I'm a plain Jane old maid.' In the following client–counselor interaction, this self-perception is challenged.

> *Sue:* I look at other people, you know, married people. Or people having fun, going on dates. I'm so plain, so boring. The original old maid.
>
> *Counselor:* I've noticed that you often refer to yourself as a 'plain old maid.' Tell me who first told you in some way that you were plain.
>
> *Sue:* Who first told me? Well, it must have been my parents, of course. I've always been ugly, even as a child. My father called me an 'ugly duckling.' I didn't mind. I was a tomboy, unlike Paula, who was really pretty.
>
> *Counselor:* So, your mom and dad first gave you the message that you were plain?
>
> *Sue:* Yes. I guess being plain looking actually saved me some of the pain Paula went through. I told you what happened because she had dates. You know I remember my mother going through the ceiling when she came home one day with make-up. My father also went wild. I remember him scrubbing it off her face.

Counselor: What do you make of that now, looking back?

Sue: Well, it fits in with what we've been talking about. Being attractive or wearing make-up gets you noticed. Our parents didn't want us noticed.

Counselor: Being a 'plain Jane' was what your family wanted you to be. It was what they expected.

Sue: Yes, but I am plain. Plain and dumpy. I did let myself get dumpy. My mother used to say heavy girls are virtuous, and 'shapely' girls are sluts. Jim tells me that I have nice eyes. That's what they tell fat people, nice eyes.

Counselor: In your family you were expected to be plain and that's how you learned to see yourself. You tried to live up to those expectations, maybe by gaining weight. Yet, those outside your family, like Jim, have seen something different, like your attractive eyes.

Sue: I can see where this is leading. I can make choices about how I look as an adult. I don't need to meet my parents' expectations. I'm not sure I believe that, but maybe I could spruce up a bit. I've lost weight since I stopped drinking and it does feel good. You also think I have nice eyes?

A similar interaction addressed Sue's perception of herself as boring. In fact, she revealed that some of her co-workers liked to talk with her at lunch because she was so well read and kept up an interesting conversation. Also, Sue had a real sense of determination, which was probably what allowed her to stop drinking and deal with the sexual abuse issue so doggedly. Through discussions in counseling she became aware of this trait, an aspect of her personality to which she had never given credence. Exploring these strengths was a fruitful endeavor for Sue.

Having made progress in dealing with self-esteem issues, Sue then focused on her interpersonal relationships, the main issue that brought her to counseling. She decided that 'risking' hurt was worth being less lonely and therefore joined an active, reputable singles' club, a major step for her. Attending the first few planned activities was very difficult for Sue, but she soon began to get to know several of the members – both men and women. Within a month of joining the club, she was asked out on a date. She began to see one of the members, Jake, on a regular basis. Shortly thereafter she became sexually active with Jake and reported no sexual difficulties. She eventually decided to end the relationship, realizing Jake had a 'drinking problem.' Although she was disappointed, she was well entrenched in the club and felt confident she would meet someone else.

Discussion

Making life changes was an important aspect of Sue's healing. Stopping drinking, feeling better about herself, and becoming more active socially were all significant changes for her. Counseling interventions that challenged Sue's negative self-views and facilitated her increased awareness of her positive self-views were used to address self-esteem issues. Supportive interventions, such as encouraging Sue to discuss her new activities, were helpful as she risked new social interactions. In this phase of counseling, Sue expressed her belief that 'things were really happening.'

Addressing resolution issues

In the final stages of counseling, Sue dealt with several resolution issues, the search for meaning being the most predominant. At this point, she claimed that she no longer hated her father, although she did hate what he had done to herself, her mother, and her siblings. Sue also reported that she no longer wished her father harm as she once had. However, she expressed a strong need to know 'why he did what he did,' so her attempt to 'understand the event: why it happened and what impact it has had' (Taylor, 1983: 1161) became the focus of several counseling sessions. In the following counselor–client interaction, Sue begins to seek an answer to this question and the counselor encourages her search:

> *Sue:* I just cannot understand why anyone would do that to his little girls. Was he sick or was he evil? He'll have to pay in hell, one way or the other. Maybe it was the alcohol. I guess it really doesn't matter, it happened.
> *Counselor:* I know I've heard you wonder before why your father did what he did, so perhaps it is an important question for you. There may not be a definite answer, and whatever the answer, the abuse was wrong. However, many individuals who have had a traumatic experience wonder why it happened.
> *Sue:* I do wonder a lot. I think about him a lot now. I know he was an alcoholic, but there are many alcoholics who don't abuse their children. I've read that sometimes those who abuse their children were abused themselves. I suspect that might be true of my father. I do know my grandfather was in jail for a long stretch. I think for assaulting someone in a bar. Maybe even for killing someone. So he could not have been a model parent. My grandmother, she was weird. She was a cold fish.
> *Counselor:* So you would guess that your father had some pretty poor parenting himself.
> *Sue:* I'm sure he did. Grandma was really weird. I wouldn't be surprised if she abused my father sexually.
> *Counselor:* That might be a possibility. Often, those who abuse others were abused themselves.
> *Sue:* You know I wouldn't be surprised if my mother was also abused.

> Both her parents died of alcoholism – you know, liver problems – so
> at the very least she probably had a miserable childhood. Us kids
> probably didn't stand a chance of getting good parents.

Sue also found meaning in her experience by coming to believe
some benefit had come from her healing process. In the following
interaction she comes to this conclusion:

> *Sue:* Now that I'm doing so well, someone asked me the other day if
> I'm glad the abuse happened.
> *Counselor:* What did you say?
> *Sue:* No, I'm not glad. This has been too painful and I lost too many
> good years of my life because of it. But, as bad as it was to be abused
> and to be a hermit for all those years, something good has come from
> this. Paula and I are close in a way we have never been before. Did
> you know I'm going to see her over my vacation? Also, now I know
> I'm strong. Everyone told me this, but now I believe it.

Relinquishing the survivor identity was also an important step
for Sue, as reflected in the following interaction with the
counselor:

> *Sue:* It's funny, for a while I didn't know I was an incest victim. Then
> for a year, it was all I could think about. I was obsessed with it. Now,
> things are good. I have other things to think about. I'll never forget
> it [the abuse], of course, but it doesn't rule my life.
> *Counselor:* Yes, your abuse is an important part of your history but due
> to your strength and all the work you've put into dealing with it, it
> no longer guides your life. You've moved beyond thinking of yourself
> primarily as an incest survivor.

Shortly after this interaction, Sue decided to end counseling. She
spent several more sessions reviewing her progress, stating future
goals, and saying goodbye to the counselor. She stated that she
believed that she would continue to expand her circle of friends
and was contemplating beginning college. She visited her mother
periodically but was no longer her 'caretaker.' Although she was
sad and a 'bit scared' to be ending counseling, Sue believed she had
made significant progress and stated that she now felt 'healthy.'

Discussion

Counseling interventions that validated Sue's need to search for
meaning were important in this stage of counseling. For Sue, this
search involved deciding why her father had abused her, so exploring possible causes of his abusive behavior (e.g. his own childhood
abuse) enhanced the resolution process. The counselor also
facilitated discussion of two other important resolution issues for
Sue: finding benefit from her healing experience (e.g. her strength,
her close relationship with Paula) and giving up the survivor role.

Appendix
An Unsent Letter

Dear Mom

I write this to you as a 33-year-old man who has been through many years of therapy; has had two wives, both of whom left me; and years of battling obesity and impotence. It is only within the last year that I realize much of this has to do with the years you sexually abused me by having me sleep with you and have sex with you. I know Dad was a horrible man, and his abuse contributed to my problems, but that was no reason for you to get your 'needs' met by me. That was not fair.

I thought I was such an oddball. Until recently I really believed I was the only one in the whole world who had sex with his mother. To me that was the most shameful thing a 'man' could do. I never thought it was abuse because I thought males could not have sex unless they really wanted to. I believed I was a pervert. Now I know that what happened was your responsibility – not mine. You were the mother, the adult. You stimulated me. I responded probably as any boy would.

I regret your life was so empty you turned to me like you did. I now know you were mentally ill. That does not excuse what you did but I do forgive you somehow. I've gotten on with my life, and have even lost 80 pounds. Once I was able to stop thinking of myself as a real deviate I could move on. I've done that. I hope you find peace.

Your son,
William

References

Abramson, L., Seligman, M. and Teasdale, J. (1978) 'Learned helplessness in humans: critique and reformulation', *Journal of Abnormal Psychology*, 87: 49–74.

Agosta, C and Loring, M. (1988) 'Understanding and treating the adult retrospective victim of child sexual abuse', in S. M. Sgroi (ed.), *Vulnerable populations: Vol. 1. Evaluation and treatment of sexually abused children and adult survivors*. Lexington, MA: Lexington Books. pp. 115–36.

Allen, C. V. (1980) *Daddy's girl*. New York: Berkeley Books.

Angelou, M. (1971) *I know why the caged bird sings*. New York: Bantam Books.

Armstrong, L. (1978) *Kiss daddy goodnight*. New York: Pocket Books.

Bass, E. and Thornton, L. (eds) (1983) *I never told anyone: Writings by women survivors of child sexual abuse*. New York: Harper and Row.

Benward, J. R. and Densen-Gerber, J. (1975) 'Incest as a causative factor in antisocial behavior: An exploratory study', *Contemporary Drug Problems*, 4: 323–40.

Blake-White, J. and Kline, C. M. (1985) 'Treating the dissociative process in adult victims of childhood incest', *Social Casework: The Journal of Contemporary Social Work*, 66: 394–402.

Blume, E. S. (1986) 'The walking wounded: post-incest syndrome', *Siecus Report*, 15: 5–7.

Brady, K. (1979) *Father's days*. New York: Dell.

Briere, J. (1989) *Therapy for adults molested as children*. New York: Springer.

Briere, J. and Runtz, M. (1988) 'Post sexual abuse trauma', in G. E. Wyatt and G. J. Powell (eds), *Lasting effects of child sexual abuse*. Newbury Park, CA: Sage. pp. 85–99.

Britcher, J. C. (1986) 'Rape and incest: the long term effects on victims'. Doctoral dissertation, United States International University, 1986. *Dissertation Abstracts International*, 46: 4449–50B.

Browne, A. and Finkelhor, D. (1986) 'Impact of child sexual abuse: a review of the research', *Psychological Bulletin*, 99: 66–77.

Bruckner, D. F. and Johnson, P. E. (1987) 'Treatment for adult male victims of childhood sexual abuse', *Social Casework: The Journal of Contemporary Social Work*, 68: 81–7.

Carlson, S. (1990) 'The victim/perpetrator: turning points in therapy', in M. Hunter (ed.), *The sexually abused male: Vol. 2. Application of treatment strategies*. Lexington, MA: Lexington Books. pp. 249–66.

Carmen, E., Rieker, P. R. and Mills, T. (1984) 'Victims of violence and psychiatric illness', *American Journal of Psychiatry*, 141: 378–83.

Chodoff, P., Freidman, S. B. and Hamburg, D. A. (1964) 'Stress, defenses and coping behavior: observations in parents of children with malignant diseases', *American Journal of Psychiatry*, 120: 743–9.

Cole, C. L. (1985) 'A group design for adult female survivors of childhood incest', *Women and Therapy*, 4 (3): 71–82.

Cole, C. H., and Barney, E. E. (1987) 'Safeguards and the therapeutic window: a group treatment strategy for adult incest survivors', *American Journal of Orthopsychiatry*, 57: 601–9.

Daugherty, L. B. (1984) *Why me?* Racine, WI: Mother Courage Press.

Davis, L. (1990) *The courage to heal workbook*. New York: Harper and Row.

Draucker, C. B. (1989) 'Cognitive adaptation of female incest survivors', *Journal of Consulting and Clinical Psychology*, 57: 668–70.

Draucker, C. B. (1992) 'The healing process of female adult survivors: constructing a personal residence', *Image: Journal of Nursing Scholarship*, 24 (1): 4–8.

Draucker, C. B. (in press) 'Finding positive meaning in a negative experience of incest', *Western Journal of Nursing Research*.

Ellenson, G. S. (1988) 'Detecting a history of incest: a predictive syndrome', *Social Casework: The Journal of Contemporary Social Work*, 66: 525–32.

Erikson, E. (1968) *Identity: youth and crisis*. New York: Norton.

Evans, M. C. (1990) 'Brother to brother: integrating concepts of healing regarding male sexual assault survivors and Vietnam veterans', in M. Hunter (ed.), *The sexually abused male: Vol. 2. Application of treatment strategies*. Lexington, MA: Lexington Books. pp. 57–78.

Faria, G. and Belohlavek, N. (1984) 'Treating female adult survivors of incest', *Social Casework*, 65: 465–71.

Farmer, S. (1989) *Adult children of abusive parents*. Chicago: Contemporary Books.

Finkelhor, D. (1979) *Sexually victimized children*. New York: Free Press.

Finkelhor, D. and Browne, A. (1985) 'The traumatic impact of child sexual abuse. A conceptualization', *American Journal of Orthopsychiatry*, 55: 530–41.

Finkelhor, D. and Russell, D. (1984) 'Women as perpetrators: review of the evidence', in D. Finkelhor (ed.), *Child sexual abuse: New theory and research*. New York: Free Press. pp. 171–87.

Finkelhor, D., Hotaling, G. T., Lewis, I. A. and Smith, C. (1989) 'Sexual abuse and its relationship to later sexual satisfaction, marital status, religion, and attitudes', *Journal of Interpersonal Violence*, 4: 379–99.

Finkelhor, D., Hotaling, G. T., Lewis, I. A. and Smith, C. (1990) 'Sexual abuse in a national survey of adult men and women: prevalence, characteristics, and risk factors', *Child Abuse and Neglect*, 14: 19–28.

Forward, S. and Buck, C. (1978) *Betrayal of innocence: Incest and its devastation*. New York: Penguin Books.

Gelinas, D. J. (1983) 'The persisting negative effects of incest', *Psychiatry*, 46: 312–32.

Gerber, P. N. (1990) 'Victims becoming offenders: a study of ambiguities', in M. Hunter (ed.), *The sexually abused male: Vol. 1. Prevalence, impact, and treatment*. Lexington, MA: Lexington Books. pp. 153–76.

Gil, E. (1990) *Treatment of adult survivors of childhood sexual abuse*. Walnut Creek, CA: Launch.

Gold, E. R. (1986) 'Long-term effects of sexual victimization in childhood: an attributional approach', *Journal of Consulting and Clinical Psychology*, 54: 471–5.

Goodman, B. and Nowak-Scibelli, D. (1985) 'Group treatment for women incestuously abused as children', *International Journal of Group Psychotherapy*, 35: 531–44.

Gordy, P. L. (1983) 'Group work that supports adult victims of childhood incest', *Social Casework: The Journal of Contemporary Social Work*, 64: 300–7.

Greenwald, E. and Leitenberg, H. (1990) 'Post-traumatic stress disorder in a non-clinical and nonstudent sample of adult women sexually abused as children', *Journal of Interpersonal Violence*, 5: 217–28.

Gross, R. J., Doerr, H., Caldirola, D., Guzinski, G. M. and Ripley, H. S. (1980) 'Borderline syndrome and incest in chronic pain patients', *International Journal of Psychiatry in Medicine*, 10: 79–96.

Hall, L. and Lloyd, S. (1989) *Surviving child sexual abuse.* New York: Falmer Press.

Hathaway, S. R. and McKinley, J. C. (1967) *The Minnesota Multiphasic Personality Inventory Manual.* New York: Psychological Corporation.

Herman, J. L. (1981) *Father–daughter incest.* Cambridge, MA: Harvard University Press.

Herman, J. L. and Hirschman, L. (1981) 'Families at risk for father–daughter incest', *American Journal of Psychiatry*, 138: 967–70.

Herman, J. L. and Schatzow, E. (1984) 'Time-limited group therapy for women with a history of incest', *International Journal of Group Psychotherapy*, 34: 605–15.

Herman, J. L. and Schatzow, E. (1987) 'Recovery and verification of memories of childhood sexual trauma', *Psychoanalytic Psychology*, 4: 1–14.

Herman, J. L., Russell, D. and Trocki, K. (1986) 'Long-term effects of incestuous abuse in childhood', *American Journal of Psychiatry*, 143: 1293–6.

Hunter, M. and Gerber, P. N. (1990) 'Use of terms victim and survivor in the grief stages commonly seen during recovery from sexual abuse', in M. Hunter (ed.), *The sexually abused male: Vol. 2. Application of treatment strategies.* Lexington, MA: Lexington Books. pp. 79–89.

Ingram, T. L. (1985) 'Sexual abuse in the family of origin and unresolved issues: a gestalt/systems treatment approach for couples', *Family Therapy*, 12: 175–83.

Jacobson, A. (1989) 'Physical and sexual assault histories among psychiatric out-patients', *American Journal of Psychiatry*, 146: 755–8.

Jacobson, A. and Herald, C. (1990) 'The relevance of childhood sexual abuse to adult psychiatric inpatient care', *Hospital and Community Psychiatry*, 41 (2): 154–8.

Jehu, D., Klassen, C and Gazan, M. (1986) 'Cognitive restructuring of distorted beliefs associated with childhood sexual abuse', *Journal of Social Work and Human Sexuality*, 4: 49–69.

Johanek, M. F. (1988) 'Treatment of male victims of child sexual abuse in military service', in S. M. Sgroi (ed.), *Vulnerable populations: Vol. 1. Evaluation and treatment of sexually abused children and adult survivors.* Lexington, MA: Lexington Books. pp. 103–14.

Josephson, G. S. and Fong-Beyette, M. L. (1987) 'Factors assisting female clients' disclosure of incest during counseling', *Journal of Counseling and Development*, 65: 475–8.

Joy, S. (1987) 'Retrospective presentations of incest: treatment strategies for use with adult women', *Journal of Counseling and Development*, 65: 317–19.

Kasl, C. D. (1990) 'Female perpetrators of sexual abuse: a feminist view', in M. Hunter (ed.), *The sexually abused male: Vol. 1. Prevalence, impact, and treatment.* Lexington, MA: Lexington Books. pp. 259–74.

Kinsey, A. C., Pomeroy, W. B., Martin, C. E. and Gebhard, P. H. (1953) *Sexual behavior in the human female*. Philadelphia: Saunders.

Kovach, J. S. (1983) 'The relationship between treatment failures of alcoholic women and incestuous histories with possible implications for post-traumatic stress symptomatology'. Doctoral dissertation, Wayne State University, *Dissertation Abstracts International*, 44: 710A.

Landis, J. (1956) 'Experiences of 500 children with adult sexual deviances', *Psychiatric Quarterly Supplement*, 30: 91–109.

Langmade, C. J. (1983) 'The impact of pre- and postpubertal onset of incest experiences in adult women as measured by sex anxiety, sex guilt, sexual satisfaction, and sexual behavior'. Doctoral dissertation, Rosemead Graduate School of Professional Psychology. *Dissertation Abstracts International*, 44: 917B.

Lepine, D. (1990) 'Ending the cycle of violence: overcoming guilt in incest survivors', in T. A. Laidlaw and C. Malmo (eds), *Healing voices*. San Francisco: Jossey-Bass. pp. 272–87.

McBride, J. M. (1984) 'A comparative study of college women with and without incest experience in relation to self-concept and guilt disposition'. Doctoral dissertation, University of Florida. *Dissertation Abstracts International*, 45: 1920B.

McCord, J. (1985) 'Long term adjustment in female survivors of incest: An exploratory study'. Doctoral dissertation, California School of Professional Psychology. *Dissertation Abstracts International*, 46: 650–1B.

McNaron, T. and Morgan, Y. (eds) (1982) *Voices in the night: Women speaking about incest*. Minneapolis: Cleis Press.

Malmo, C. (1990) 'Recovering the past: using hypnosis to heal childhood trauma', in T. A. Laidlaw and C. Malmo (eds), *Healing voices*. San Francisco: Jossey-Bass. pp. 194–220.

Maltz, W. and Holman, B. (1987) *Incest and sexuality*. Lexington, MA: Lexington Books.

Masters, W. H. and Johnson, V. E. (1970) *Human sexual inadequacy*. Boston: Little, Brown.

Matthews, R., Matthews, J. and Speltz, K. (1990) 'Female sexual offenders', in M. Hunter (ed.), *The sexually abused male: Vol. 1. Prevalence, impact, and treatment*. Lexington, MA: Lexington Books. pp. 275–94.

Meiselman, K. C. (1978) *Incest*. San Francisco: Jossey-Bass.

Meiselman, K. C. (1980) 'Personality characteristics of incest history psychotherapy patients: a research note', *Archives of Sexual Behavior*, 9: 195–7.

Murphy, J. E. (1989) 'Telephone surveys and family violence: Data from Minnesota'. Paper presented at the Responses to Family Violence conference, Purdue University, West Lafayette, IN (January).

Olson, P. E. (1990) 'The sexual abuse of boys: a study of the long-term psychological effects', in M. Hunter (ed.), *The sexually abused male: Vol. 1. Prevalence, impact and treatment*. Lexington, MA: Lexington Books. pp. 137–52.

O'Toole, A. W. and Welt, S. R. (1989) *Interpersonal theory in nursing practice: Selected works of Hildegard E. Peplau*. New York: Springer.

Owens, R. H. (1984) 'Personality traits of female psychotherapy patients with a history of incest: a research note', *Journal of Personality Assessment*, 48: 606–8.

Peters, S. D. (1988) 'Child sexual abuse and later psychological problems', in G. E. Wyatt and G. J. Powell (eds), *Lasting effects of child sexual abuse*. Newbury Park, CA: Sage. pp. 101–17.

Peters, S. D., Wyatt, G. E. and Finkelhor, D. (1986) 'Prevalence', in D. Finkelhor (ed.), *A source book of child sexual abuse*. Beverly Hills, CA: Sage. pp. 15–59.

Ramey, J. (1979) 'Dealing with the last taboo', *Siecus Report*, 7: 1–2, 6–7.

Roland, B. C., Zelhart, P. F., Cochran, S. W. and Funderburk, V. W. (1985) 'MMPI correlates of clinical women who report early sexual abuse', *Journal of Clinical Psychology*, 41: 763–6.

Roland, B., Zelhart, P. and Dubes, R. (1989) 'MMPI correlates of college women who reported experiencing child/adult sexual contact with father, stepfather, or other persons', *Psychological Reports*, 64: 1159–62.

Rosenfeld, A. A. (1979) 'Incidence of a history of incest among 18 female psychiatric patients', *American Journal of Psychiatry*, 136: 791–5.

Russell, D. E. H. (1986) *The secret trauma: Incest in the lives of girls and women*. New York: Basic Books.

Satir, V. (1988) *The new peoplemaking*. Mountain View, CA: Science and Behavior Books.

Scott, R. and Thoner, G. (1986) 'Ego deficits in anorexia nervosa patients and incest victims: An MMPI comparative analysis', *Psychological Reports*, 58: 839–46.

Sepler, F. (1990) 'Victim advocacy and young male victims of sexual abuse: an evolutionary model', in M. Hunter (ed.), *The sexually abused male: Vol. 1. Prevalence, impact, and treatment*. Lexington, MA: Lexington Books. pp. 73–86.

Sgroi, S. M. (1989a) 'Stages of recovery for adult survivors', in S. M. Sgroi (ed.), *Vulnerable populations: Vol. 2. Sexual abuse treatment for children, adult survivors, and persons with mental retardation*. Lexington, MA: Lexington Books. pp. 111–30.

Sgroi, S. M. (1989b) 'Healing together: Peer group therapy for adult survivors of child sexual abuse', in S. M. Sgroi (ed.), *Vulnerable populations: Vol. 2. Sexual abuse treatment for children, adult survivors, and persons with mental retardation*. Lexington, MA: Lexington Books. pp. 131–66.

Sgroi, S. M. and Bunk, B. S. (1988) 'A clinical approach to adult survivors of child sexual abuse', in S. M. Sgroi (ed.), *Vulnerable populations: Vol. 1. Evaluation and treatment of sexually abused children and adult survivors*. Lexington, MA: Lexington Books. pp. 137–86.

Silver, R. L., Boon, C. and Stones, M. H. (1983) 'Searching for meaning in misfortune: making sense of incest', *Journal of Social Issues*, 39 (2): 81–102.

Sisk, S. L. and Hoffman, C. F. (1987) *Inside scars*. Gainesville, FL: Pandora Press.

Skorina, J. K. and Kovach, J. A. (1986) 'Treatment techniques for incest-related issues in alcoholic women', *Alcoholism Treatment Quarterly*, 3 (1): 17–30.

Struve, J. (1990) 'Dancing with the patriarchy: the politics of sexual abuse', in M. Hunter (ed.), *The sexually abused male: Vol. 1. Prevalence, impact, and treatment*. Lexington, MA: Lexington Books. pp. 3–46.

Swanson, L. and Biaggio, M. K. (1985) 'Therapeutic perspectives on father-daughter incest', *The American Journal of Psychiatry*, 142: 667–74.

Taylor, S. E. (1983) 'Adjustment to threatening events: a theory of cognitive adaptation', *American Psychologist*, 38: 1161–73.

Thomas, T. (1989) *Men surviving incest*. Walnut Creek, CA: Launch.

Tsai, M. and Wagner, N. N. (1978) 'Therapy groups for women sexually molested as children', *Archives of Sexual Behavior*, 7: 417–27.

Urbancic, J. C. (1987) 'Incest trauma', *Journal of Psychosocial Nursing*, 25: 33–5.

Urquiza, A. J. and Capra, M. (1990) 'The impact of sexual abuse: initial and long-term effects', in M. Hunter (ed.), *The sexually abused male: Vol. 1. Prevalence, impact, and treatment*. Lexington, MA: Lexington Books. pp. 105–36.

Urquiza, A. J. and Keating, L. M. (1990) 'The prevalence of the sexual victimization of males', in M. Hunter (ed.), *The sexually abused male: Vol. 1. Prevalence, impact, and treatment.* Lexington, MA: Lexington Books. pp. 89–104.

Van Buskirk, S. S. and Cole, C. F. (1983) 'Characteristics of eight women seeking therapy for the effects of incest', *Psychotherapy: Theory, Research, and Practice*, 20: 503–14.

Wegscheider-Cruse, S. (1985) *Choicemaking.* Deerfield Beach, FL: Health Communications.

Westerlund, E. (1983) 'Counseling women with histories of incest', *Women and Therapy*, 2 (4): 17–31.

Whitfield, C. L. (1989) *Healing the child within.* Deerfield Beach, FL: Health Communications.

Wiehe, V. R. (1990) *Sibling abuse.* Lexington, MA: Lexington Books.

Index